1

WILKINSON-LATHAM

BARCODE
OVER

CYCLES IN COLOUR

Cycles
in Colour

ROBERT WILKINSON-LATHAM

Special photography by John Searle Austin

Colour paintings by Helen Downton

BLANDFORD PRESS
Poole　　·　　Dorset

First published in 1978
by Blandford Press Ltd,
Link House, West Street, Poole,
Dorset BH15 1LL

Copyright © Blandford Press 1977

ISBN 0 7137 0853 0

For Christine and Edward

Typeset in 11 on 12 point Bembo and
printed and bound by
Cox & Wyman Ltd,
London, Fakenham and Reading

Contents

5

Illustration credits

The author and publisher would like to thank the following for their help with the colour illustrations.

Mr and Mrs Ned Passey, Benson
Members of the Benson Veteran Cycle Club
The Imperial War Museum
Nikki Leroy, Theatrical Costumier, Brighton
Raleigh Ltd
Cycles Peugeot (U.K.) Ltd
Brighton Museum

Acknowledgements

I would like to express my deep thanks to all those individuals and organizations who willingly and helpfully supplied information, references, colour transparencies or allowed the cycles in their collections to be photographed. Special mention must be made of Mr Ned Passey and his wife and daughter who so patiently and helpfully allowed John Searle Austin and myself to descend on them on a number of occasions to photograph cycles from their superb and unique collection and for supplying information about their collection. Information that Mr Passey kindly and unstintingly gave came from his deep and enthusiastic knowledge of cycles stored in his head and never was there a pause for reflection or a book opened.

I must also thank the following for their help.

John Maillard and Paul Moran of Raleigh Ltd
M. D. East of M.E.P.R., Public Relations for Bickerton Bicycles
A. J. Lauterwasser of Cycles Peugeot (U.K.) Ltd
Pat Hodgson for picture research
Miss L. Morris of the Science Museum
Mr Allan of the Imperial War Museum
Miss Caroline Dudley of the Brighton Art Gallery and Museum

7

Members of the Benson Veteran Cycle Club
The organizers and participants of the 17th Benson Annual Cycle Rally
The staff of the reference library, Brighton
Lastly many thanks to Lynda Jackson who typed the drafts and final manuscript.

Robert Wilkinson-Latham
Brighton, *January 1978*

Introduction

Possibly the earliest surviving evidence of a bicycle-type machine is a drawing by the famous artist and inventor, Leonardo da Vinci. The drawing, dated 1493 shows a far more advanced bicycle than the early hobby horses of the beginning of the nineteenth century. Both the wheels of the same size have eight spokes, the front wheel being equipped with handlebars for steering and the saddle situated over the back wheel. What was centuries in advance was the method of propulsion which consisted of two pedals fitted to a toothed gear. The chain, or whatever, over this toothed gear passed over a smaller one on the rear wheel so that the power from the rider's feet was transferred to driving the back wheel. Surprisingly, this idea was not adopted on bicycles until the 1870's.

It was not until the middle of the seventeenth century that inventors and coach builders produced a number of 'horse-less carriages' which were propelled by the driver. Johann Hautch, a famed inventor from Nuremberg, built a number of carriages of this type. It was claimed by an eyewitness that it went backwards and forwards and attained a speed of 3,000 paces an hour. The driver steered the vehicle with a lever but the power was provided by two children inside the carriage turning cranked handles! There were other examples of this type of machine, but they were essentially carriages and were slow and cumbersome. A smaller but hardly more efficient machine was invented by Dr Elie Richard of La Rochelle.

This machine was controlled by two people. The master sat inside the small carriage suitably protected from the elements by a roof and steered by means of cords attached to the front swivelling axle while the power was provided by the servant standing outside the carriage behind the protective canopy. The servant stood on two treadles and supplied the power by putting his weight alternately on them. Quite a speed could be obtained with a strong servant on the flat but lack of any braking system made it dangerous in the extreme downhill and no amount of jumping up and down by the servant could persuade the machine to tackle a hill.

The *Universal Magazine* of 1761 describes the invention of a certain Mr Ovenden which was again similar to the carriage of Dr Richard. The magazine stated that it was '. . . doubtless the best that has hitherto been invented, as it is capable of travelling with ease six miles an hour, and by particular exertion of the footman might travel nine or ten miles an hour on a good road . . . But this carriage is in general only calculated for the exercise of gentlemen in parks or gardens . . .'

In Paris, there were also inventors at work on these two main velocipedes, M. Blanchard and M. Masurier. It was basically on the Richards style and Blanchard, an inventor and balloonist extraordinary as well as a great publicist was in 1799 ordered by royal command to demonstrate his machine before Louis XVI in the courtyard of Versailles. However, to get full impact for his machine the inventor demonstrated it in the Place de Louis XV and after several circuits sped off to keep his royal appointment. In 1793, he travelled to America and in Philadelphia gave some demonstrations. It was during one of these meetings that he met Benjamin Franklin. In 1805 one of his letters reveals his infinite faith in his machine. 'I once drove Doctor Franklin,' he wrote, 'from Paris to Versailles in 1 hour 45 minutes . . . and I have had the honour of taking the Queen and certain Ladies for rides in the Park at Versailles, and I also drove my carriage up the ramp in front of the Opera at Versailles which is impossible even for the best horses.' However, no one seemed very impressed with the machine and it soon faded and disappeared.

By this time (1805), however, a far more simple yet more far-reaching machine had been seen in Paris. This, the true forerunner of the bicycle rather than the manumotives mentioned above appeared first in 1791 in the gardens of the Palais-Royal. It was driven by the famous French eccentric, the Comte de Sivrac, and took the form of a small carved wooden horse fitted with wheels propelled by the movements of the legs alternatively in a similar fashion as running. There was no steering and corners could only be negotiated by the rider leaning over in the direction which he wished to take. It is doubtful if Sivrac was the inventor of this machine as smaller horses similar to this had for some years been children's toys. The machine was named the 'Célérifère'. The new machine immediately caught on and soon numbers of Incroyables were to be seen scudding around the gardens of the Palais-Royale to catch the eyes of the prostitutes who sat there or paraded in the arcades. In 1793, the machine was renamed the Vélocifère and enjoyed immense popularity but rather than a machine of practical use, they were purely of a fashionable one. The bodywork was by no means exclusively horses and some were fitted with carved lion's heads. The popularity of the machine led rise to a number of satirical cartoons as well as a comedy produced at the Vaudeville Theatre in 1804 entitled 'Les Vélocifères'. The natural progression amongst the young men was to form a club and this they did at the turn of the century. They organized races up and down the Champs-Élysées where the main object was the winning of money either as a rider or from placing bets. A contemporary French newspaper, *Le Siècle* recorded in 1802 that 'Outside a well-known café in the Boulevard des Italiens, a number of races were organized to the Rue Royale and the Champs-Élysées. However, the most important races were offered to the young aristocrats of the time and betting was

11

lively'. Racing must have been precarious as not only did the machine have no steering or brakes but the uneven road surface must have claimed many a casualty to the delight of the onlookers.

By this time, however, the machine had been slightly redesigned and renamed the céléripède. This was an improved model, usually without the trappings of the fake horse but still with no steering column with which to turn the front wheel. This redesign allowed a more comfortable saddle to be used as well as shedding the superfluous weight of the wooden horse. The new machine had the two wheels connected by struts to the simple crossbar that ran the length of the machine and on which the rider sat. But during the first decade of the new century, the fad quickly faded as all fashion does and it was not until the restoration of the monarchy in 1816 that another attempt was made to resurrect the céléripède. This was done by none other than Nicephore Niepce of Châlon-sur-Sâone, perhaps better known as the leading light behind the invention of photography. In 1816, the resurrected machine differed slightly in construction but was once again an object of fashion rather than practical use.

It was in the following year that Charles, Baron von Drais de Sauerbrun of Mannheim 'invented' a machine of practical use. He dispensed with the ludicrous horse-like image of the previous machines and substituted a triangular wood frame with two struts at the back and front to hold the wheel and he introduced a steering system to control the front wheel. Besides that, he also included a padded armrest on the steering bar so that greater purchase could be obtained with the feet over rough ground. The machine later called the 'Draisienne' was constructed for a purely practical purpose, the Baron being not only an engineer but Master of the Woods and Forests of the Grand Duke of Baden and therefore needing a suitable method of conveyance while carrying out his functions. The machine although it had been mentioned in German newspapers in 1817 was first demonstrated

12

in public in Paris where it attracted some attention. However, a contemporary newspaper wrote that 'This machine can never be of any real utility as it can only be used in a garden or park or a well kept road'. The Baron was not to be deterred and he gave other demonstrations of his machine, the most convincing being in Germany, the newspapers reporting that he cut 2 hour journeys on foot to a single hour when riding.

A ladies' version was produced in 1819 but it was viewed solely as a pastime rather than as a practical means of transport for ladies. In 1819, Ackerman's *Repository of Arts and Science* states, concerning the Draisienne that, 'A person who has made himself tolerably well acquainted with the management of one can, without difficulty urge himself forward at the rate of eight, nine or even ten miles an hour. In one account we are informed that experiments have shown it to be easy to travel fifty miles a day on these German hobbies... The price, we are informed, varies from eight to ten guineas, and their whole weight does not exceed fifty pounds.'

The popularity of this improved machine soon meant that it was introduced into other countries namely England, Germany and even as far as the United States of America. In England it was copied by Denis Johnson of Long Acre in London who was a coachmaker. He patented the machine and renamed it the Pedestrian Curricle. Once more the machine as it had done previously appealed to the fashionable 'Dandies' or the 'Corinthians' of the Regency period as it had done to the 'Incroyables' in France. The popularity was immense and they were soon a common sight in London. Special riding schools were established to teach the art of riding as with horses and Denis Johnson while not only making the machines was quick to establish a large school where the aristocrats were taught to ride. Not content with manufacturing and selling them and teaching the new owners, he also hired out machines to those who could not afford the £8–£10 required. The *London Magazine* of 1819 however, pointed out that Johnson was on to a good thing as the machines he sold for those high prices cost him no more than about 'forty or fifty shillings'.

In America, W. K. Clarkson imported the idea and obtained a patent in 1819 but unfortunately his enthusiasm was greeted with little interest and no great general use of it ensued. It was used by some for exercise in parks but failed to gain the popularity it had in Britain and Europe.

Because of this popularity in Britain the 'Hobby Horse' or Draisienne became the object of the satirical cartoons so loved at this period and even the Prince Regent did not escape ridicule. The caricature depicting the Prince shows two hobby horses with the Prince and a military officer both lying full length face down in a state of some intoxication with 'ladies' mounted on their backs driving them on. The interesting feature on the print is that both the Prince and the officer *seem* to be propelling the front wheel with their hands on rudimentary cranks. However, on closer inspection, these seem to be foot rests or even artistic licence as a convenient place to put the hands. Cartoons of this nature abounded attacking the hobby horse, one famous one being 'The Hobby Horse Dealer' showing some Regency bucks examining a hobby horse as they would a real one while in the background the horses look on with apprehension with a sign above their stables stating that 'A fine stud of REAL HORSES to be sold as cheap as dog meat ...'

The claims that these machines could be propelled at speeds of up to 10 miles an hour was seen by many as a danger to life and limb especially in the crowded Metropolis and so under the Paving Act, they were banned, but whether this was upheld rigorously or not is not known and only a handful of convictions were ever made.

But while there were those that condemned the hobby horse there were others who advocated its usefulness. An anonymous writer in the *Gentleman's Magazine* of 1819 who described himself as 'Speedy-Pace' suggested that the hobby horse was suitable for tradesmen who have to travel as well as servants carrying messages and for doctors in rural areas. However, before the hobby horse craze slowly faded, improvements had been made to these crude machines. The most notable was that of Louis Gompertz in 1821. His invention relied on the old method of foot power being replaced by arm power. The Gompertz machine was unchanged in appearance except that in place of the previous steering bar, he fitted a cross bar with two connecting rods on the end of which was a toothed quadrant which engaged a pinion on the hub. The action of pulling the bar back and forth made the quadrant act on the hub and turned it. To enable the machine to be more efficient he added a padded chest rest above the saddle.

Interest in the hobby horse foot propelled or otherwise dwindled and by the late 1820's and 1830's there were exceptionally few in use and even fewer interest in developing the idea of two-wheeled travel. Most of the inventors of this period were channelling their ideas into three- and four-wheeled horseless carriages. These and other weird inventions are described in Chapter III. In 1839, however, a Scottish blacksmith named Kirkpatric Macmillan produced the first pedal-driven bicycle in a forge at Courthill in Dumfriesshire.

1

The First Pedal Power and the Boneshaker

add in with drawing of the state of the cycle but on page 17

Macmillan was not only an excellent craftsman but something of an inventor and had a local reputation for turning his hand to anything including improving the horse-drawn plough. He had seen an ordinary hobby horse brought to the forge by a local gentleman presumably for repair and he and a fellow smith named John Freeman decided to make copies of it for themselves so that they could ride them on the estate of the Duke of Buccleuch for whom they worked. Rather than make a straight copy, Macmillan decided on some refinements and on one great improvement. The refinements included a better-designed frame of a single piece of wood shaped from high at the front and then sweeping down and then slightly up again where the frame forked to take the rear wheel. The saddle was fitted on the downward curve and behind it, because of the larger size of the rear wheel, a protector to stop the wheel touching the driver. Handlebars were fitted to the front and according to the copy made by

Thomas McCall who built it in 1860 from the original drawings for James Johnston of the Glasgow Cycling Club, he could not resist placing a small carved wooden horse's head at the front. The wheels were of wood and shod with iron tyres and the machine of course possessed no brakes. The great step forward was however, the fitting of pedals or more correctly treadles. Bars were fitted each side of the top of the frame beneath the handlebars and descended to a suitable level and a foot rest fitted. These bars at the front were connected with rods to cranks on the back axle. The backward and forward movement of the treadles were therefore transmitted to the rear wheel and turned it.

To ride the machine, Macmillan had some special boots with spikes on the sole (this was not a new idea as a London bootmaker had produced iron-clad soles for hobby horse riders during the Regency) as these allowed him to get the machine underway by the old hobby horse method. Once reasonable speed was obtained, the feet were lifted from the ground and placed on the treadles and worked back and forth. Although the machine had steering it must have been very slight as any major movement would have entangled the wheel with the treadle rods. Macmillan, however, seemed greatly pleased with the bicycle and was often to be seen in the local vicinity driving around.

On 6 June 1842, he set out on a monumental (for those days) journey from Courthill to Glasgow and back. Whether this was for publicity (which he certainly got), for necessity or pleasure is not known. He arrived in Glasgow the following day and immediately attracted large crowds. In the Gorbals, because of the number of people who had turned out, he accidentally knocked down a small child. Fortunately the child was not injured but Macmillan was summoned to the local Police Court and fined 5/- (25p) for reckless driving. A local paper carried an account of the journey describing how he had covered 40 miles in 5 hours, erroneously attributing the speed of the machine to wheels turned by

17

hand and ending up stating that 'This invention will not supersede the railway'.

However, the news of the machine remained local and in none of the London learned journals was there any mention of it. Neither did Macmillan seek or want publicity for his machine and he never took out a patent for it. He was not interested either in making it for others. A number of local craftsmen made copies of his machine to which he had no objection but as he had no patent there could be little objection. One such man was Gavin Dalzeel, a cooper from Lesmahagow situated between Courthill and Glasgow. He may well have been inspired by the sight of the machine when Macmillan made his famous journey, but whatever, he did build a copy in about 1846. In the 1860's, Thomas McCall of Kilmarnock built several of these machines as, it seems, a commercial venture. These were now fitted with brakes, better steering, alterable connecting rods for long or short legs – all for the price of £7.

Despite Macmillan's place as the inventor of the bicycle there does remain the machine constructed by E. M. Artamonov, a Russian serf. This machine was meant to have been constructed in 1801. It had a large front wheel and a small back one like the later Penny-Farthing, and was driven as the later ordinaries were by pedals fitted to the large front wheel. However, despite this claim, it does seem highly unlikely that the date of this 'invention' is correct.

However, for the next few decades, the bicycle, despite activities of a certain few and until recently of ignored inventors, was to take a back seat to velocipedes of three or more wheels. Those that were actually made with two wheels were either impractical, useless or no improvement on what Macmillan had accomplished. One such machine, that of Richard C. Hemming of New Haven, Connecticut, U.S.A., known as the Hemmings Unicycle, had as its name suggests a single wheel with the cyclist sitting inside it. This machine, said to attain 25 miles per hour was propelled by a combination of foot and hand power. Other examples of these three- and four-wheeled machines are described in Chapter III.

The first two-wheeled pedal-driven bicycle produced commercially was made in Paris by Pierre and Ernest Michaux, father and son. They conceived their first prototype in 1861 from an old Draisienne they were repairing for a Parisian hatter M. Brunel. After one or two attempts they eventually arrived at the simple expedient of fitting two cranks, one each side of the hub of the front wheel and attaching wood pedal blocks to them. And so was born the first pedal-driven bicycle. However, the true inventor of the pedal bicycle is in dispute although rather neatly tied up by the modification and experimentation of the old Draisienne delivered for repair. This is not unique to bicycles and many inventions are clouded with legend and myth over the years which makes it impossible or nearly so to unravel the web to find the truth. A contractor to the Michaux concern who specialized in the manufacture of perambulators, invalid and three-wheel velocipedes, named Pierre Lallement – a coachbuilder, who worked briefly for the firm had also been independently experimenting. His first appearance was in 1861 when accompanied by his manservant, who was equipped with roller skates, he rode around the Place de la Concorde. Lallement, however, took out patents on his invention which Michaux either failed to do which is surprising or was beaten to it, which is more likely. Lallement who now worked for Michaux received little credit, it all going to Michaux and – disgusted by the lack of recognition – the former left France in 1863 and went to America, the land of opportunity where he hoped for great things. Establishing himself in Ausonia, Connecticut, he waited the statutory two years before taking out the first bicycle patent in 1866 in conjunction with J. Carrol of Newhaven, Connecticut. However instant success was not to be his and being impatient and hearing of the great success of the Michaux he returned to France in 1867.

However, the father and son Michaux had already gone ahead with the commercial production of their 'invention' and in 1863 made and sold 142 machines. *The Times* in London however, was not particularly impressed and described this machine as the 'new terror of the streets' which is hardly surprising when from old photographs one sees the mixture of traffic and the congestion in London, for example, at this time. By 1865, the production of the Michaux bicycle had risen to 400 and three years later a new factory was opened employing nearly 300 workmen who produced five machines a day. The success of the Michaux venture stimulated inventors and the *English Mechanic* which was founded in 1865 had its columns full of ideas, and drawings from inventors. The bicycle had its advocates but there were those who considered it yet another whim of the industrialized and mechanical age in which they lived and after all this new-fangled machine on which the rider did all the work cost as much as a horse!

However, Michaux père et fils were not concerned, they could not make enough bicycles and soon established like Johnson had done previously a riding school to teach the 'art' and ran a hire service for those unable to afford the cost. Michaux's machine was not only popular in France but it was copied in Munich in Bavaria in 1862. Had Lallement stayed longer in the United States he may well have made his fortune for what was termed by the press as 'Velocipedomania' seized such respectable cities as New York and Boston, with manufacturers springing up, riding schools becoming established and the Patent Office in Washington being besieged with inventions. In 1869, it was noted that there were 400 machines waiting to be examined for patents and each week over eighty applications were received for either new machines or improvements to existing patents.

The bicycle or as it was soon to be known, the 'boneshaker', was a simple machine, not far advanced, except for the mode of propulsion from the hobby horse. It was however, not entirely made from wood as the previous machines had been. The Michaux machine was made in a combination of wood and metal. The frame was made from wrought iron diamond section bar which formed a fork section at the rear to accommodate the wheel (slightly smaller in diameter to the front wheel) while the front wheel fitted with brass bearings was placed between a fork which was in its turn fitted to the frame so that it could turn from side to side. To give the rider some form of comfort, if it could be called that, considering the road surfaces at that time, the saddle was fitted on a leaf spring which stretched from the steering column by a lug and was fitted with a fork at the rear and bolted to the hub of the back wheel. A brake was fitted which worked on the back wheel which was 'activated' by a rotary movement of the handlebars which tightened the cord working on the brake. Finally the machine was fitted with a mounting step on one side.

Like other items of the day, finish could be ordered to the customers' wants and the cycles ranged from 350 to 500 francs in price. Even while Michaux, the 'inventor' seemed to have the monopoly, other manufacturers sprang up all over France and elsewhere. In France there were firms such as Oliver Frères, Tribout and Mayer, all of Paris, Truffault in Tours and Rousseau in Marseilles. Also in Paris was Michaux's arch-rival Lallement who had formed on his return from America the 'Ancienne Compagnie Velocipedienne' implying in the name that he was the first and oldest manufacturer.

The Americans were not slow either in exploiting this new craze, for exploiting the hobby really was the aim rather than the desire to establish an organized industry. In 1869, Pickering and Davis of New York were actually exporting bicycles to England and other firms soon sprang up in New

York and Boston. In New York were Mercer & Monod, Calvin Whitty, the Hanlon Brothers and the Wood Brothers while in Boston the manufacture of bicycles was in the hands of the Kimball Brothers and William P. Sargeant & Co. Other inventors and small manufacturers also contributed to the mania that pervaded these two cities, many of them filling patent after patent with their so-called 'improvements'. Calvin Whitty however, was probably more a businessman than most. He investigated the Patent Office archives and found that Lallement had filed the first bicycle patent and promptly purchased it from the Frenchman for $2,000. He then embarked on sending out letters to all manufacturers informing them that they were infringing his patent. He offered them the choice of paying $10 royalty per machine or a law suit. Until the end of the mania, Whitty probably made more in royalties than he did from manufacturing machines of his own. However, as quickly as it came, the fashion disappeared, but not before riding schools had been set up and prospered and gymnasiums hastily converted to cater for this boom in trade. In Boston, alone there were twenty schools for cyclists all of them open 24 hours a day to cater for the large numbers of 'students'. A contemporary American Journal, the *Scientific American* was all in favour of the bicycle and stated that 'The advantages . . . are obvious. It takes men from the bar-rooms into the pure air, into God's light and sunshine . . . and furnishes a means of healthful, invigorating and pleasant exercise'.

As in other centres where this machine was popular, it was not purely considered a machine for getting from A to B, and various feats were performed upon it. Most of these either in America or France took the form of juggling or some other acrobatic display and even races. But these were not held in America, because suddenly in 1871, the velocipede was dead, killed possibly by the commercial greed of manufacturers and the fact that it was treated as it had been done earlier in France as a fad or fashion rather than as a serious means of propulsion. It was considered in America as a toy whereas in France and shortly in Britain it was considered a worthwhile and useful machine, capable of many applications and providing a means of transport which was self-reliant.

In 1868, on 31 May at Saint Cloud near Paris, the first bicycle race on a track specially designed took place. This was over a distance of 1,200 metres and was won by an Englishman, James Moore, who lived in Paris and had been taught to ride by Michaux. The first long-distance race was held the following year on 7 November 1869 between Paris and Rouen over a distance of 83 miles. Of the entries which numbered over 200, five were women on their 'boneshakers'. The winner in a remarkable time considering the machine and road conditions was again James Moore who accomplished the journey in 10 hours and 25 minutes.

The seriousness with which the French and soon the British would treat this machine led to the formation of cycle clubs, the first being 'Le Veloce Club de Paris' and the publication of a magazine catering for the sport, *Le Velocipede Illustré*. Besides this, the first all-cycle show was held in Paris in 1869 which showed to the public the various wares of the makers, two-wheeled, three-wheeled and some with even more wheels. Wheels were now fitted with spokes, tubular metal frames, some with solid rubber tyres or treads replacing the iron-shod wheels, an elementary form of springing on the front wheel to help cushion the driver against the bad road conditions and a brake. Another innovation shown was the mud guard to protect the dress of the wearer when passing through wet and muddy conditions.

In France and in other countries notably Britain, cycles had been constructed for 'ladies' to use but they were deemed a toy or plaything and were not taken seriously. Those that constructed machines for serious use were hampered by accepted codes of dress and so as in horse-riding and hunting, these machines were made side-saddle. Plates 22 and 26 show two versions of the side-saddle, the second plate being of a later vintage. However, these machines must have been difficult to control and propel.

A breakthrough to what was later called rational dress when cycling really caught on with women was the 'invention' of the 'Bloomer', pantaloons inspired by Eastern dress. It first appeared in Semaca Falls in New York State and despite its dubbed name was first donned by Mrs Miller and not by Mrs Amelia Bloomer. In France, however, this type of garb soon caught on with the mania for the cycle. Plate 16 depicts a French lady rider of about 1868 showing a scandalous amount of leg. But this was not to be all, for in the same year, a ladies' cycle race was held. In this instance Mademoiselle Julie beat Mademoiselle Louise by half a wheel, with some skirts flying and legs exposed or wearing bloomers if we are to believe the spirited engraving that appeared in *Le Monde Illustré*. All contestants, however, observed some propriety and wore hats suitably adorned with feathers.

France, at this time was years ahead of any other country in cycle development but the looming war clouds gathered fast and in 1870, France and Prussia were at war. Although cycle production resumed after the war and the French defeat, Britain had forged ahead, while in America, the mania had disappeared.

In Britain until the late 1860's two-wheeled machines had largely been ignored or dismissed as impractical and emphasis placed on machines with three or more wheels. The real start of the two-wheeled bicycle as a viable and popular machine was given by Rowley B. Turner, who was a student in Paris and agent for the Coventry Sewing Machine Company. Rowley had been interested in bicycles when the gymnasium of a M. Cuissard established a company in his name for the manufacture of 'boneshakers'. Business boomed, as with all cycle makers in France and soon he found it necessary to sub-contract parts to keep up with the orders. Because of the company's manufacturing problems, R. B. Turner contacted his uncle, Josiah Turner, who was the manager of the Coventry Sewing Machine Company suggesting that he should make 'boneshakers' which could be sold in France. He travelled over to England in the same year bringing with him one of his machines which he rode in London to Euston Station where he travelled north to Coventry. At Coventry he collected his machine from the guard's van and rode to the works of the Coventry Machine Company at Cheylesmore. At the factory, R. B. Turner was quick in persuading his uncle and James Starley, the foreman at the works to manufacture a special order for him of 400 machines. The factory at that time was low on work and despite some preliminary objections from the shareholders, launched into full production in February 1869. At the same time the name of the company was changed to the Coventry Machinist Co. Ltd. However, before the initial order could be completed, war had broken out in France and these 'frustrated exports' were put on the British market.

This 'launching' of the cycle in earnest on the British market was precipitated by Turner's appearance again in London where he demonstrated a machine at the gymnasium of Charles Spencer. After his impressive show, he persuaded Spencer to become an agent and to devote part of his gymnasium to a riding school. Amongst his spectators was the famous photographer John Mayall and after some preliminary lessons, Spencer, Rowley and Mayall cycled round Trafalgar Square and then set off towards Brighton. Previous to this Mayall had attempted a solo run but only got as far as Redhill when having demonstrated his machine to the railway staff he took the train back to London. On the second run, he was more successful and in fact arrived first. *The Times* correspondent who followed the three in a carriage and pair reported that 'They kept pretty well together as far as Crawley, after which Mr Mayall took a decided lead, and arrived in Brighton in time and in good condition for dinner, and the second part of Kuhe's concert in the Grand Hall'.

Spencer and Rowley, however, it seems did not possess the stamina and finished the ride in a coach with presumably their machines unceremoniously bundled and tied on top. Mayall had covered the distance in 16 hours. Two months later, however, C. A. Booth covered the distance in 7½ hours.

Snoxell and Spencer, the firm in which Spencer was a partner encouraged by the publicity soon set themselves up as sellers of cycles, although they advertised themselves (the laws on advertising were less strict then) as manufacturers. Charles Spencer soon produced a manual for those who wished to study the subject. He not only advocated the type of machine desirable (usually one he sold) but also the riding dress which included a flannel guernsey, drawers, serge trousers, half-wellingtons and a buttoned serge jacket. One stipulation was that the clothing was to be in a dark colour because of having to oil the machine and that the boot should have thick soles as walking up hills was unavoidable.

Charles Spencer went on to great things. He claimed to have taught Prince Albert how to ride, became President of the Middlesex Bicycle Club and in June 1873 was one of a party that rode from London to John o' Groats in 2 weeks.

By March 1869, the cycle mania gripped London and other cities and towns, Liverpool being in the forefront. The 'Thunderer' (*The Times*) boldly announced in its edition of 24 March 'A New Terror in the Streets'. It followed this with 'We are already beginning to taste the first fruits of velocipedomania. A summons ... was issued at Clerkenwell Police Court against a "comic singer" for driving a velocipede along the foot pavement at the rate of 10–12 miles an hour ... he knocked down three persons, ran over the foot of another, attempted to escape and was with difficulty captured by the police. If this is the kind of thing we are to expect from velocipedes a pleasant prospect is opened for the pedestrians.'

In May 1868, the first cycle track race was held in Britain at Hendon and the trophy won by Arthur Markham. In the following year on 17 May a new machine appeared at the Crystal Palace at Sydenham at the International Velocipede and Loco machine Conference by W. F. Reynolds and J. H. Mays of Tower Hill in London. This machine was named the 'Phantom'. Reynolds and Mays were proprietors of the 'Phantom' and Carriage Wheel Company Ltd of 10 King Street, Tower Hill, London. Their machine was a revolutionary step forward in cycle design. The 'Phantom' won a prize. The frame of the machine was constructed of iron rods and was hinged in the middle. This innovation allowed the steering to be done by both wheels and gave a smaller turning circle. If somewhat difficult to manoeuvre with this hinged frame which never became popular the 'Phantom' did have spoked wheels. These primitive spokes consisted of wire attached to one side of the hub, through an eyelet in the rim to the other side of the hub. There were fifteen 'spokes' per wheel. To obtain the necessary tension, the hub was made in two parts which were wedged together after the wheel had been made. The wheel also had a solid rubber tyre fitted to it. This innovation caught on rapidly and within three years, the wood wheel for the cycle had disappeared in favour of this new pattern. An added advantage was that this machine weighed only 53 lbs.

Another not insignificant development had also taken place in most machines. This was the increasing size of the front wheel. Although not vastly larger as in the later 'Ordinaries' or Penny-Farthings, the front wheel of most machines was appreciably larger. This came about because of the mode of direct propulsion. The larger the wheel then the more distance was covered in a single turn of the front wheel. This theory was to be taken to absurd lengths during the 1870's before the gear, the chain- and shaft-driven machine was invented.

The bicycle craze had gripped the country by 1869 and besides the Coventry Machinist's Company, there were also ten makers in London, ten more in Wolverhampton and at the beginning countless blacksmiths and coachbuilders, who made the component parts and sold them to small manufacturers, unable to afford plant and machinery. Enthusiasts who preferred to build their own 'boneshaker' were all enthusiastic buyers of parts, adding perhaps one or two ingenious improvements of their own.

2

Ordinaries and 'Dwarf' Ordinaries

Although the boneshaker continued to be manufactured until about 1872, its popularity had been on the decline for a number of years. The most significant factor behind this decline in popularity, apart from the road surfaces, was that it needed considerable leg muscle power to drive the machine for any distance. Horses and horses and carriages were easier and required very little effort. It seemed that unless an improvement could be made, the bicycle was doomed to fade into obscurity. However, there was an answer and this was supplied by a number of makers and enthusiasts, but perhaps the greatest contribution to the cycle was made by James Starley – the 'Father of the Cycle Industry'.

The introduction of the larger front wheel which enabled a rider to cover more ground with a single revolution of the pedal was thought to have been made by Magee in Paris in 1869; the machine having a front wheel of 48 ins and a rear wheel of 24 ins. The development in France of this design of machine might have gone on further had not the Franco-Prussian War broken out. As it was, it was in England that the further evolution of the bicycle took place. James Starley was the foreman of the Coventry Sewing Machine Company which in 1868 changed its name when it took to manufacturing the Michaux style of velocipede to the Coventry Machinist Company. At a young age when working on his father's farm just outside Brighton, he had invented a number of improvements and later when employed as a gardener to John Penn he not only invented and improved machinery but took an interest in most things mechanical.

As foreman at the works, he introduced such small refinements as the mounting step on the boneshaker, but best of all he saw the practicability and greater efficiency of the larger wheel and the infinite possibilities of gearing.

In 1871, Starley who had by now left the Coventry Machinist Company formed a partnership with William Hillman, the founder of the motor car company that bears his name, to sell their latest design of bicycle, the 'Ariel'. The 'Ariel' was a unique machine incorporating iron frames and wheels fitted with tangential spokes. These ribbon spokes which were adjustable were firstly made from sheet brass, then strips of steel and finally round metal wire. Individual adjustment of the spokes was not possible and a device fitted to the hub with adjustable tie rods enabled all spokes to be adjusted at the same time.

However, Starley and Hillman did not have the field to themselves for in the same year William Grout, a cycle maker of Stoke Newington produced his so-called 'tension' bicycle. This machine was similar in design to the 'Ariel' with the large front wheel and the smaller rear steadying wheel but the main and important difference between the two lay in the design of Grout's wheels. The spokes on the Grout machine were individually fitted into adjustable nipples in the rim of the wheel which made it now possible to adjust individual spokes. Grout's machine also had a new design of pedal. Another improvement of Grout's was having the front forks of the cycle hollow thus reducing the weight.

Within two years, the boneshaker was outmoded and used

purely either to learn on or by those with insufficient finances to be able to afford a new machine but who could afford to buy the second-hand boneshakers that now came on to the market at ludicrous prices in their thousands.

The original 'Ariel' and Grout machines had a front wheel of about 48 ins in diameter and a rear wheel just over 24 ins, but models were soon available with front wheels up to 60 ins in diameter. These however, could only be ridden by a very tall thin man. The usual size, however, for the front wheel was about 54 ins.

The 'Ariel' in 1871 when launched sold for £8 but with Starley's speed-gear the price was £12. This invention of Starley's enabled the front wheel to revolve twice for a single revolution of the pedals. But neither Starley nor Grout or even any other of the manufacturers were prepared to rest on their laurels and in 1873 Starley patented his tangent spoking for wheels which is the method still in use today. Starley's method was to set the spokes in the rim at a slant so that they crossed each other and provided extra tension, and strength.

By the mid-1870's it was estimated that there were nearly 50,000 'ordinaries' by various makers on the roads, but despite its popularity, the new bicycle was by any standards not the ideal machine. While speeds never before dreamed of could be obtained on it, it was unstable, difficult for the novice and dangerous for both novice and experienced hand alike. Coupled with these drawbacks was the dislike of the cyclist by the general public, and in many parts of the country, poor roads which doubled the risk of a fall off these machines. Many complaints were received from horse owners that these infernal machines frightened horses and because the by-laws varied in all parts of the country, police and magistrates interpreted the law with a bias against the cyclists who were considered as deserving of no leniency if they would ride at a furious pace, swerving in and out of the traffic and being a general nuisance and danger to the public. The public dubbed them with such names as 'cads on castors'.

31

Little boys delighted in upsetting these 'cads' by the simple expedient of pushing a stick through the spokes as the machine passed by. Other accidents were unavoidable such as dogs running out, bad road surfaces and inexperience on a machine with no brakes, a high and unstable driving position and a vulnerable thin wheel rim and tyre.

There are one or two recorded deaths of cyclists who crashed their 'ordinaries'. *The Times* for 24 May 1884 recorded a fatal accident when a cyclist in attempting to avoid a small boy swerved and as the newspaper states 'his foot got entangled in the wheel, causing him to pitch head-foremost into a ditch by the roadside. In his descent his right eye came in contact with the branch of a tree'. While fatal accidents were few, cyclists took a frequent 'header', 'Imperial crowner' or 'cropper' usually caused if not by children or animals but by objects such as a small piece of coal dropped from the coal merchant's cart or even a stone in the bad road surface. The conditions of most roads were bad for cyclists as maintenance consisted of dumping the necessary filling material in the hole and leaving the passage of carts to level the surface. Many accidents happened in this way and the cyclist had little or no redress against local authorities. If the work on the road done by the authority was shown to be negligent then the cyclist could sue because of 'mis-feasance' but if the authority neglected to do the work even though legally bound the cyclist had no redress because it was deemed 'non-feasance'.

The life of the cyclist was often dangerous and many if not most formed themselves into cycling clubs, not only for enjoyment but also in some small way for protection – safety being in numbers. Perhaps the most vicious attack on a cyclist happened in August 1876 when a group of cyclists were heading along the high road at Hendon when they were overtaken by the St Albans coach. The driver and guard had obviously brushed with cyclists before who had the habit of racing coaches much to the annoyance of the driver and occupants because they were suitably armed to attack these 'cads on castors'. The guard, a Henry Cracknell had provided himself with a large iron ball on the end of a piece of rope. This missile was launched by the guard at the secretary of Trafalgar Bicycle Club and at the same time for good measure, the driver named Parsons lashed out with the whip. The unfortunate cyclist was overturned with his machine and dragged some distance behind the coach until the rope broke.

In court, the full story was told. The Secretary of the Club had, he admitted, sworn at the driver for not allowing him to pass while the driver calling on past experiences of cyclists frightening his horses admitted to taking preventive action. The magistrate, however, refused to accept the driver's story and fined him £2 and the guard £5. There was, as can be imagined, an uproar in the cycling fraternity. The *Bicycle Journal* thundered that 'We think to charge £5 for the chance of killing a man is holding human life too cheap'.

The growth of cyclist clubs was stupendous. From 1870 with the founding of the first club, the Pickwick Bicycle Club in Hackney, the numbers increased to thirty-one in Britain, seven of which were in London by 1874 and 2 years later the total clubs in the country had increased to fifty-seven. By 1878 the number of London clubs had risen to sixty-four and elsewhere to 126. In 1884, however, when the mania had taken full grip, the total number of clubs in Britain amounted to 534. On a national level the Bicycle Union was formed in 1878 and the Bicycle Touring Club as well. This later in 1883 changed its name to the Cyclists' Touring Club and in 1886 boasted some 22,000 members.

Besides the problems mentioned above, it was the police who posed the worst threat to the cyclists. In London many summonses were taken out against cyclists for 'furious riding' and some outlandish speeds were attributed to the cyclist by the constable on the beat who had arrested them. The favoured area in the 1880's was Kensington and Hammersmith because of the wood paving on the road which gave an excellent riding surface. Fines differed greatly and for the same offence one cyclist on one day was fined £2 (the maximum) while another in front of a different magistrate was fined only £1. Policemen, however, were also to blame as they had no training in trying to gauge speed. To emphasize this lack of training and also to highlight some of the speeds attributed by the police to riders in December 1881, *Wheel World*, alluding to the Hammersmith magistrates court, published a satirical article about a case at 'Sledgehammersmith' Police Court. In evidence against some cyclists who were charged with 'Furious riding' a police constable giving evidence stated that the defendants were riding at 40 miles an hour; however, he walked after them, overtook them and took them to the station in handcuffs! Another officer called who stated he was 'on patrol in the London Dock area' added that he saw the defendants in Hammersmith riding at 500 miles an hour!

The cycle boom that occurred in Britain was not just a fad but was as a result of high-powered publicity by the manufacturers. This publicity took the form of road racing and speed trials and each manufacturer was anxious to obtain the leading rider for their escapades. Starley with his 'Ariel' was one of the first to indulge in this form of publicity and together with his partner Hillman they attempted and completed a ride from London to Coventry. They took their machines to Euston by train and after an overnight stay set off early the following morning. By one o'clock they had covered nearly half their journey and near Bletchley had lunch and rested for an hour before continuing. The only mishap on the entire journey was when Hillman took a 'header' when the tyre came off the front wheel. They arrived in Coventry after night had fallen but had completed the 96 mile journey in the time.

In 1873, the famous racing cyclist J. Moore recorded a speed of $14\frac{1}{2}$ miles an hour on an 'Ariel'. Not to be outdone, Thomas Sparrow, a London cycle maker with a Piccadilly showroom and wealthy clients to match, decided on an even greater publicity stunt. He financed four riders to cover the journey from London to John o' Groats, a distance of 861 miles. These intrepid cyclists completed their gruelling journey in 2 weeks averaging, as the *Daily Telegraph* pointed out 60 miles a day. 'To say that the work would tire a horse,' the newspaper continued, 'is a feeble description of it. The strongest horse would *break down* under such a journey.' Besides the tests sponsored by manufacturers, clubs organized outings and inter-club competitions. Some publications devoted to cycling and cyclists gave advice to those planning a continental trip as well as the necessary advice on the most suited cycle clothing, for cycling was a serious business. To cater for this specialized clothing certain bespoke tailors added to their range and advertised themselves as cyclist tailors. While at some considerable cost they provided the club outer garments, there were many who gave advice as to what the ideal undergarments should be. The undergarments it was advised should fit closely to the body and should be of pure wool. Great care was advised with the flannel shirt to make sure that the maker's label and neck band in linen were not present because if they became damp and the wind got up, they could be the cause of severe chills. Great care was also advised in inspecting the work of the tailor, especially the outer garments to make sure that the linings were wool and that canvas had not been used in stiffening the bands of the trousers.

The Cyclists' Touring Club advised the following outer garments. To get the greatest possible wear from the jacket it was recommended that it be braided inconspicuously on the inside although some clubs as part of their 'uniform' incorporated braiding on the outside. The colour of the outfit was all important and the Cyclists' Touring Club recommended a small checked Tweed which was designed not to show the dust. Others preferred darker colours that would not show oil stains.

	s.	d.	
Jacket	32	0	(£1.60p)
Breeches or knickerbockers	16	0	(80p)
Waistcoat	10	0	(50p)
Shirt	11	6	($57\frac{1}{2}$p)
Gaiters	8	6	($42\frac{1}{2}$p)
Soft knockabout helmets	4	6	($22\frac{1}{2}$p)
Helmets	6	6	($32\frac{1}{2}$p)
White straw hats ... with			
registered ribbon. Complete	4	6	($22\frac{1}{2}$p)
Straw hats with ribbon	3	6	($17\frac{1}{2}$p)
Registered ribbon	2	0	(10p)
Polo caps	2	9	(14p approx)
Deerstalker or wideawake	5	9	(29p approx)
Puggarees for helmet	2	0	(10p)
Stockings	4	0	(20p)
Gloves	3	3	($16\frac{1}{2}$p approx)
Silk handkerchiefs or			
Mufflers in club colours			
... registered 14 ins square	6	6	($32\frac{1}{2}$p)

No well-heeled cyclist could afford to be seen not wearing the 'regulation' outfit of his club.

While the clubs organized themselves and organized outings, the manufacturers who were now increasing at a furious pace still continued to publicize their wares by speed trials, races and endurance journeys, but perhaps the most popular of all was cycle racing. As in modern racing, it allowed designers to try out and test their ideas, it allowed and nurtured development and improvements and it proved beyond doubt to would-be purchasers the reliability of the machine. Racing against others or against the clock was a popular sport of the 1870's which drew enormous crowds and established idols and heroes amongst the athletes who established records and broke others' records.

However, before looking at the records established by these men on their high machines it is as well to examine the difficulty in mounting let alone controlling an ordinary. Charles Spencer, one of those who completed the London to John o' Groats ride, published in 1877 a manual entitled *The Modern Bicycle* which was the what to do and what not to do for the ordinary. After discussing the suitable wheel size according to height Spencer explains the method of 'mounting' the machine.

'The saddle being nearly as high as your shoulder it is impossible to vault on; but a step is fitted on the backbone at a convenient height on the left. It is jagged to afford a firm grip for the toe. There are two ways of mounting. One is to start the machine and run by the left side, and put the toe upon the step while in motion, throwing the right leg over on to the seat; the other is to stand at the back of the machine with the left toe on the step and to hop with the right leg until you have gained a sufficient impetus to raise yourself on the step, and throw your right leg across the seat.

The first is the best plan. In many cases it is the only practicable way, as for instance, for remounting on a slight ascent, where it would be most difficult to get up sufficient speed by the hopping plan. This, moreover, does not present a very graceful appearance.

Hold the handle with the left hand and place the other on the seat. Now take a few running steps, and when the right foot is on the ground give a hop with that foot, and at the same time place the left foot on the step, throwing your right leg over on to the seat. Nothing but a good running hop will give you time to adjust your toe on the step as it is moving. It requires, I need not say a certain amount of strength and agility.

In alighting by the step all you have to do is to reach back your left foot until you feel the step, and, resting upon the handles, raise yourself up and throw the right leg over the seat to the ground. But I consider getting off by the treadle much the preferable way when you can manage it. First see that the left hand crank is at the bottom, then throw your right leg with a swing backwards and continue until your are off the seat and on the ground. As it is, of course, easier to get off the slower you are going, you must come almost to a standstill just keeping way enough to prevent the machine falling over. If you attempt it when going at all quickly, you will have to run by its side after you are off, which is a difficult feat for any but a skillful rider.

The great advantage of getting off in this way is that you can choose your own time, which is very useful when an obstacle suddenly presents itself, as in turning a corner. In getting off the other way you are liable to lose time feeling for the step.'

The racers, so beloved by the cycling public, had established a number of records which when one considers the machine they were riding and the exertion necessary to propel it and balance it, let alone attain high speed with it, were quite outstanding. James Moore had, as we have seen already established himself as a champion in 1869 but other records were soon to be set up. At the Lillie Bridge track in October 1874 David Stanton beat a rival in a 106-mile race with a time of just under 8 hours. In 1878, F. Smyth in spite of adverse conditions of wind and rain and bad roads drove 218 miles in 24 hours. By the following year however, the mile had been ridden in just under 3 minutes and in 1882, H. L. Cortis completed a trip of over 20 miles in 1 hour.

All this publicity stood the manufacturers in good stead. There were over fourteen in Coventry in the mid-1870's and the numbers blossomed elsewhere. There were such names as the Coventry Machinist Company, who later altered their name to the Swift Cycle Company and there was T. Humber established in Nottingham, John Keen who had his factory at the Angel Inn, Thames Ditton in Surrey, Dan Rudge in

Wolverhampton, George Singer in Coventry (one of the many in the city) and a number of others. Many of the concerns which established themselves as cycle manufacturers did not however make all the parts and bought in some from the larger concerns to keep the cost down. By the end of the decade the cycle had because of the foresight of a number of makers and experience on the track, been improved. In 1876, John Keen had invented the stub axle for the rear wheel which lightened the machine by doing away with the fork while the following year most manufacturers adopted the 'Stanley' steering head perfected by the Sheffield manufacturers Hydes and Wigfall. The same year ball-bearings were introduced to replace the old-fashioned brass bushes in the front and rear wheels. These bearings came in various forms as inventors and manufacturers patented what they thought was an improvement. There was Rudge with the double-cone ball-bearing and Starley's odd-shaped rollers spaced apart by smaller ones. By the end of the 1870's the ordinary had reached its peak of perfection with hollow drawn front forks, steel tubing used in the frame for weight reduction and other perfections. Although by the early 1880's the popularity was on the wane it took a further 10 years before the manufacturers of the ordinary ceased.

But before the ordinary passed from the scene, its fame had spread elsewhere and most importantly to America. The ordinary was probably first seen by the general American public at the Continental Exposition in Philadelphia in 1876 and a retired military man Colonel Albert A. Pope having seen the machine, visited London and Coventry to study the method of construction. Returning to the States he set up a manufactory at Hertford, Connecticut, which produced its first machine in 1878, in a converted sewing machine factory. There were no other manufacturers that rivalled Pope – although various firms imported English machines – until 1886 when a machine known as the 'Victor' was produced by the Overman Wheel Company of Boston. Pope was, however, a man with foresight and considerable organizing skill and he produced what is considered to be the first production line and it was said that later when Henry Ford undertook the manufacture of his famous Model T he adopted and adapted Pope's ideas of a production line. Pope, like his English counterparts was also a publicist and he hired the famous 'boneshaker' champion William Pitt to demonstrate his 'Columbia' ordinary but although the rider was arrested after the machine had frightened a horse before the ride got underway, the invited press men gave an immense amount of publicity to the event. Pope went on to foster and encourage racing and also was instrumental in getting roads improved. Even so, cycling was in its infancy in America because of the state of the roads even in places such as San Francisco and Boston where the first cycle clubs were formed.

Pope was however, not to be discouraged and nor it seems was a young reporter named Thomas Stevens. Besides being an eccentric, Stevens was also a bit of an explorer and presumably encouraged by Pope undertook an amazing round the world journey between 1884 and 1887 on, not surprisingly enough, one of Colonel Pope's 'Columbia' ordinaries. He set off from San Francisco on 22 April on the machine with a 50 in. front wheel, suitably kitted out with a spoke cyclometer, spare spokes, extra tyre, 20 yards of rope, a can of machine oil and cement for the tyres. As an afterthought a 'bicycle camera' was sent to him via Calcutta and he also sported amongst his equipment a suit of 'gossamer rubber'. On 10 May he encountered and shot a mountain lion in the United States but by the second week in May had arrived via Liverpool and a drive to the south coast of England and ferry, in Paris. A week later he was riding through Germany and by the beginning of June had entered Austria and Hungary arriving in Bulgaria by 24 June. In just under a month he had arrived in Istanbul from where he pushed on to Persia where he spent some 6 months.

Refreshed at the end of March 1886, he pushed on to Afghanistan where he was arrested and returned to Persia. In the heat, he found that his machine upturned and adorned with his 'gossamer' suit made a marvellous tent. By the beginning of August he was in India and over 2 months later he was near Canton in China. Passing through Japan he took the Pacific mail steamer from Yokohama bound for San Francisco. His journey inspired others at a later date to undertake similar endurance trips, the most famous being the ride of John Foster Fraser during the mid-1890's who completed a round the world trip of 19,237 miles in 774 days, but it was a less spectacular arduous and dangerous journey than Stevens had undertaken.

While makers lightened and perfected their ordinaries others were tinkering with new designs for improved performance and stability. One such man was W. S. Kelly, an American, who patented his improved 'Star' cycle in 1881 which was manufactured by the Smith Machine Company of New Jersey. Like a number of other designers of the mid-1870's Kelly's search for a safer machine involved in reversing the wheel, having the larger wheel at the back and the smaller one at the front. While this may seem a logical step to take, one must remember the reason for the large front wheel, being that of more ground covered by a single turn of the pedals. In 1869, Thomas Wiseman sent details of his machine to *English Mechanic* who published an engraving of this strange invention. The machine while still possessing a larger front wheel than back was lower on the ground than the ordinary and had front wheel propulsion but rear wheel steering. The seat was strategically placed to enable the rider to mount before moving off and as the magazine reported the rider could '. . . without dismounting, stop and shake hands with a friend'. Frederick Shearing of Norfolk also invented a machine far more advanced. This had a smaller front wheel and a larger back wheel with front wheel steering and the saddle situated over the rear wheel. The unusual feature was that the back wheel was driven by a rotary transmission and although chains were available at the time, the machine used a cord or strap possibly similar to the thousands in use in factories in those days for driving machines. Neither of these machines appeared to be commercially made. Henry Lawson was another inventor who channelled his thoughts into producing a safer machine and produced a machine which was an ordinary in reverse with steering on the smaller front wheel, the saddle situated between the two wheels and therefore nearer the ground and the propulsion was by means of pedals which worked on long thin cranks to the back wheel hub.

Other inventors and designers however left the ordinary as it was but contrived by various means involving moving the saddle farther back to make the machine safer. One of the most serious rivals to the ordinary was the 'Xtraordinary' made by Singers. This machine together with the 'Facile' (mentioned below) were patented in 1878 and posed a serious commercial threat to the ordinary. The 'Xtraordinary' placed the saddle slightly farther back than usual and to enable the rider to reach the pedals employed levers and links. However, one main criticism was that the pedal described an oval rather than a circle which some riders it appears, found disconcerting.

The 'Facile' bicycle went one better by reducing the front wheel to a mere 42 ins, placing the saddle back slightly and employing pedals, which were lowered and worked on levers which were mounted below the hub. These levers were pivoted at the front end to a specially extended front end fork and joined to the cranks by short links. The machine, although it did not appear until late 1878 had in fact been patented in 1869 by John Beale. The machine was manufactured by Ellis and Co. of Fleet Street, London and like other manufacturers and agents set about establishing their machine by endurance tests.

One of their advertisements of 1884 shows the steady whittling down of a 13-day record for a journey between

Land's End and John o' Groats established in 1880 for the feat recorded on one of their machines in 1884 when J. Adams on a 'Facile' with 46 in. diameter front wheel completed the journey in 6 days 23 hours and 45 minutes, a total of 924 miles at an average of 132 miles a day. Ellis also organized other feats of endurance and reliability and in 1882 organized a 24 hour road race, the winner W. Snook covering $21\frac{1}{2}$ miles in the allotted time. J. Adams, the champion of the previously mentioned long journey was employed as a 'work's driver' by Ellis and went on to beat a number of records culminating in a 24 hour record of $266\frac{1}{2}$ miles in 1884.

But while manufacturers advertised their victories it was certain to others that the ordinary and the so-called 'dwarf' ordinaries had reached their zenith and little improvement could be made on existing designs. To produce the perfect safety cycle needed a new approach to design and a new method of harnessing and using human leg power to propel a machine more efficiently. It was obvious that gearing was to play an important part but an improved method of transmitting the power from pedals to wheel had to be found. Some, as we shall see were already on the right track but it took the nephew of James Starley – John Kempt Starley – to furnish the answer.

3
Quadricycles, Tricycles, Tandems and Others

The tricycle was, until the advent of the safety bicycle, the most serious rival to the two-wheeled machine. It was more stable, provided women with elegant transport and could be ridden by two if so designed. As we have seen, the earliest machines designed for ladies had at least three and more often four wheels.

The main advantage of the tricycle or the quadricycle was that they required no skill at all for balancing. One mounted the machine, preferably on a flat surface, and moved forward at whatever pace required. Some of these earlier greater than two-wheeled machines designed by William Sawyer had the front wheels larger than the back ones. Sawyer issued a catalogue in 1858 extolling the fact that he had '... after 20 years of careful study and personal labour, succeeded in bringing these carriages to a perfection of ease, rapidity, lightness and durability – combined with cheapness – defying all competition ...'. Sawyer, according to his business cards counted amongst his illustrious clients such exalted persons as the Emperor of Russia and declared himself under Royal and Imperial patronage. Sawyer's machines have a special place in the development of the more than two-wheeled machines as he was a perfectionist and a craftsman and his machines – those that survive – reflect this attention to detail. The Great Exhibition of 1851 gave enormous impetus to the Sawyer machines.

His idea, was however not new. Early machines intended most especially for ladies were described as being '... admirably adapted to meet the requirements of elderly gentlemen, ladies and timid or nervous persons'.

During the 1860's Sawyer reigned supreme as the supplier of the four-wheeled machine and found his clients amongst the elderly and the females who for one reason or another, mainly social, drove slowly around to be seen. While manufacturers tried to tempt the lady riders to purchase their more sedate machines, little came of it and the most the machines could attain was as a conveyance at spas. This machine became fashionable for those 'taking the waters' and was designed like a bath chair with two rear wheels and a steering wheel at the front with a wicker chair for the rider who propelled the machine by means of foot-operated rods and cranks.

These tricycles, quadricycles or velocipedes, as they were known, were not exceedingly popular and very few were made. One such example, not made by Sawyer was the machine built in 1851 by J. Ward, a coachbuilder of Leicester Square, London, for Prince Albert. This rather heavy four-wheeled machine had a central seat over the rear pair of wheels with a central steering bar operated by an upright handle which connected to the front wheels. The machine was powered with two treadles fitted to cranks and by a forward and backward movement of the feet, the wheels were turned. Although this type of machine was never made in any quantity it still persisted in the background of cycle development and perhaps the last type to be made was the Rudge 'Triplet', a three-seater machine which appeared briefly in 1888.

Other four-wheeled machines that were made or designed were eccentric by any standards, perhaps the best example being the Celermane which carried five men. The designer, one feels, must have been a keen oarsman for the four-wheeled machine had four men, two facing forward and two aft with the cox at the back and they 'rowed' the machine, by pulling back and forth on bars connected to the wheel driving rods. An illustration of this machine appeared in *English Mechanic* in September 1869.

The largest number of more than two-wheeled machines fall into the tricycle category, and were responsible for the later cult of 'Sociable' cycling which became exceedingly popular.

The first tricycles were in effect modified boneshakers with the addition of an extra rear wheel and an axle. Yet another variation was the two-seater tricycle, one unique example has the front passenger steering and the rear passenger, probably a servant doing the pedalling with his hands on cranks.

It was not, however, until 1876 that tricycles were commercially produced for an increasing market. The driving force behind the production of these types of machines was as can be expected James Starley. His first success was with the Coventry Lever Tricycle which made its appearance in 1876.

However, before Starley put his machine on the market it had been preceded by the Dublin tricycle. This machine had a large single rear wheel with two smaller wheels at the front. The propulsion was by means of wood treadles which worked levers and rods attached to cranks on the rear wheel and in front of the rear wheel in the centre of the machine was mounted the seat. This seat with flat base and back was mounted on coiled springs for a more comfortable ride. As a tricycle it was a unique design in that it had, when viewed from the front, a large wheel on the right hand side and two small ones on the left. Drive was effected on the large wheel and steering on the two smaller ones. The initial model was

46

propelled by levers and cranks but this was later altered to the new and more conventional chain drive. The steering was also improved. In place of the earlier bath chair type steering with a single rod with grip controlling direction, he introduced a system using rack-and-pinion. This form of rather odd-looking machine became popular for about 10 years under the name of the Coventry Rudge tricycle and between 1880 and 1890 the most popular machine of this type was the Rudge Rotary.

The apparent success in the development of the tricycle led other manufacturers to enter the field. The improvements in this form of machine were made by Starley in 1879 who, taking the Coventry tricycle and adding another large driving wheel, turned the machine into a quadricycle. The seating arrangement was altered allowing two persons to be transported. Each passenger had their own set of pedals and cranks which powered the individual driving wheel by chains. Well pleased with his efforts, so the story goes, he and his son William took the machine on a run. To Starley's dismay he found that the younger man, William, exerting more force on the pedals, propelled his driving wheel at a faster speed than he himself could do thus making the machine veer to the side of the weaker man. This prompted Starley to think of a way to equalize the revolutions of the driving wheel and in 1877 he took out a patent for a bevel-gear differential unit. Starley was not himself the inventor of the differential, one patent having been taken out as early as 1828 in France, but he was the first to apply it to the tricycle. The system adopted by Starley had the axle in two parts joined with a unit of bevel wheel and pinions which allowed equal power to reach both driving wheels but had the added advantage that in cornering, one wheel, the outer one, rotated faster than the inner one. A machine incorporating this system was brought on to the market in 1877 by Starley and named the Salvo quadricycle. The machine was in fact a tricycle as Starley removed one of the smaller central wheels and provided an arm with a minute wheel as a steadying agent. At first this was at the front but soon after he reversed the order and had the balancing wheel placed at the rear.

The name of the machine was soon, however, to be changed to the 'Royal Salvo' because in June 1881 Queen Victoria ordered two of these machines. Unlike the machine mentioned above this was a single seater with a single chain drive on the left-hand wheel but, of course, with the Starley differential this did not affect the performance of the machine. The story goes that Queen Victoria was first interested in the machine at Osborne on the Isle of Wight when her carriage was overtaken by one of Starley's machines driven by a young lady. The young lady was, however, the daughter of Starley's agent who was encouraged to ride the machine for publicity purposes. The Queen, impressed by the machine and the fact that it was driven by a female demanded a demonstration at Osborne and ordered two machines. One of the conditions, so the story goes, was that the inventor was to deliver the machine himself and Starley left behind his impressions of the meeting in a letter to his wife.

'Two of her Indian servants were standing nearby and one of her ladies just behind her. I could see that tricycle under a tree and a lady and gentleman looking at it. My gentleman told me to wait a minute where I was and he went up to the Queen and bowed. She looked up and said something and he backed away a few paces and came to fetch me. She said: "We are very interested in your tricycle Mr Starley. The Prince Leopold thinks he may soon be able to ride one. You see His Royal Highness examining it now." And then he came over to stand by the Queen and she said to him, "this is Mr Starley who invented the tricycle" and he was most pleasant and asked questions about my other inventions.

I was quite overcome and bowed so low that I nearly

48

toppled over as I said "I am very honoured, Ma'am". Then the gentleman led me away and I was surprised and pleased when the Prince came along and asked me to explain the working of the tricycle, to him. A servant was wheeling it behind. We found a nice level drive where I got on and was soon rolling along in fine style. He seemed very pleased with it and thanked me very kindly.'

The publicity Starley received was overwhelming, and he, as already stated, dubbed his machine the Royal Salvo. Besides the 'royal' machine, his sons – Starley died in 1881 soon after his visit to Queen Victoria – advertised other variations on this basic form. The central gear machine was in essence the Royal Salvo but with a central chain drive to a central cogged differential on the axle while the tandem was the same machine but adapted for two riders one behind the other but with a return to the chain drive on the left hand wheel. Another variation was the Osborne, similar to the Royal Salvo but with minor variations.

While the bicycle still reigned supreme and it was difficult for manufacturers to tempt their customers to buy a tricycle, many for whom the bicycle had been an impossible or dangerous means of transport rejoiced in this safer means of transport. Before the beginning of 1880, tricycles had caught the imagination of the public to an extent where there were twenty types being manufactured, most if not all stemming from the original Starley design. Perhaps one of the major influences in the acceptance of tricycles especially for ladies was Queen Victoria, although she never rode one herself but by ordering two from Starley she 'approved' of the machine for women and this caused an upsurge in the 'sociable' type of machine where man and woman sat side by side. Gentlemen on the other hand preferred the tandem arrangement on tricycles, being more sporty and speedier.

With every new form of machine, racing and speed trials

were inevitable and some manufacturers produced special lightweight racing models. There was no doubt about it that the tricycle and even the quadricycle were more sedate and stable machines and seemed to be the preferred mode of locomotion of doctors and clergymen although even amongst those august professions there were always the radicals! The tricycle, however, had many more applications than the bicycle and for trade and commerce it proved invaluable as a delivery vehicle. By the mid-1880's they had been adapted as conveyances for chimney sweeps, dairies, newspaper deliveries and even the Post Office in 1886 adopted these machines, suitably adapted to deliver parcels. The *Evening Standard* bought from Singers a special machine known appropriately as the Carrier, to deliver newspapers to the vendors in the streets of London (Plate 63).

Because of this popularity amongst a certain element of society for the tricycle, other companies started to manufacture them, including Doubleday and Humber, the Leicester company who produced a front steering machine in 1881 and the varieties of 'sociables', either side by side or tandem. Of the many varied machines on the market, one of the most popular was the Quadrant produced in 1882 on the patent of W. J. Lloyd. The Quadrant had two large rear wheels with a central saddle and pedal arrangement with chain drive to the axle with a sturdy frame, bicycle type steering and a smaller front wheel provided with a mud guard. Another machine was the 'Demon' Hill Climber, a product of the National Works, Coventry, which had two large front wheels with the driver pedalling them directly seated over the axle with a long tail like frame with smaller rear wheel. The advertisements of this company (which boasted fresh testimonials daily) challenged any other tricycle manufacturer to ride up a flight of stairs of their showrooms in Spon Street, Coventry, and the advertisement showed a convincing illustration of a gentleman performing this feat. One testimonial about this machine from a noted member of the Midland Union of

Scientific and Natural History Societies claimed that he found the 'Demon' had many advantages namely . . . '. . . the absence of chain and cogs lessens the weight, does away with just those parts that are always getting out of order in tricycles, and a constant expense, while the machine is simplicity itself.' Fortunately this slight retrograde step in the history of cycles was never taken up in large numbers and, while probably quite adequate at climbing stairs, could never hold its own on the open road with the geared and chain-driven machines.

Another favourite machine was the tandem Humber with two large front wheels with the saddles one behind the other. The gentleman who rode behind did the steering with a conventional bicycle system and pedalled while the lady sat at the front holding on to two hand grips and pedalling as well. The manufacturers had thoughtfully provided a chain guard on the front set of chains to protect the lady's dress. A small balancing front wheel was also provided. One of the improvements incorporated in a number of designs was the clutch action, a sort of elementary free wheel which allowed the feet to be kept still while coasting. This refinement was, however, only fitted to the pedals which the lady in the pair was expected to operate.

Perhaps one of the strangest machines was the Premier Tandem Dwarf Safety Roadster (a popular name for machines) made by Hillman and his partners in 1880. This, while appearing like a safety had a precariously balanced front saddle supported, one hoped, by the small guiding wheel and limb at the front. This was, in spite of the small front wheel, a bicycle using tricycle ideas. It was never successful being a hybrid between the two types of machines.

It seemed at one time that the tricycle, the tandem and sociable especially were becoming more popular than the bicycle itself. This phenomenon, as we have seen, came from the 'sociable' aspect of the machine, the fact that it was quite acceptable for a lady to saunter slowly with her husband or paramour on one and that it was easy to ride and respectable to be seen on. Tandem riding also carried this social acceptance. When one examines the bicycles that were available it can without much effort be seen why this three-wheeled form of machine gained acceptance and popularity but the tricycle makers were soon to be in for a rude shock.

With the 'safety' machine which was applicable to both men and women, which appeared in the 1890's the tricycle declined in popularity, although smaller models continued and still continue to be produced for children.

The introduction of machines for children began earlier and in the Brighton Museum, there is a 'Boneshaker' for a child. This is rather the exception and most parents waited until the tricycle came on the market before introducing it to their children. A number of plates (69, 70 and 71) show children's tricycles which the manufacturers hoped would find a good market in cycling families, which undoubtedly they did.

The tricycle still maintained its popularity despite criticism and such machines as the Premier Racer with the three wheels the same size was liked both on and off the track. This type of machine was popular amongst the individual cyclist but when a machine was required for two, there was immense discussion about the merit of the side by side 'sociable' and the tandem machine. Practicability dictated that the tandem should win. It did not have the large wheel-base of the 'sociable', was easier to store and a lot faster on the road, although romantics declared that it was not a true 'sociable' as the riders were not side by side.

While most tricycle makers stuck to the fairly conventional layout there were others who felt they had an innovation to offer, the foremost being the machine built in 1881 by Ideal and known as the Hen and Chickens. This was a suitable name when one considers the design of the machine. It employed a large central wheel with around it and at every corner a smaller wheel. While it might have been the most stable machine on the market, it was unacceptable when it came to width. The theory behind the machine was that the four smaller outer wheels acted as stabilizers but once the cyclist was moving the drive being provided by the central wheel – the smaller wheels were clear of the ground – but unfortunately the road surfaces being what they were it was the four outer wheels or some of them which had more contact with the road than the driving wheel.

In 1884, the Humber 'Cripper' tricycles were introduced named after the maker, Humber and the racer who was a consistent winner on that machine, R. Cripps. The machine was perhaps the most popular tricycle, coming commercially on to the market in 1886 and rendering all other designs obsolete. The machine had a front wheel and fork similar to a safety machine which provided steering and braking and two wheels at the rear. The drive was by means of pedals working a cogged wheel and chain to an axle at the rear with a differential. Starley, not to be outdone produced the 'Psycho' machine which was similar in design. It took only a few more years for the rear wheels to be reduced to the same size as the front wheel and the modern tricycle was established.

Manufacturers were, however, not content to stand still and as well as making a single seater model, once more launched into the 'sociable' or tandem market. The 'one behind the other' machines were immensely popular.

In tricycles, the Humber 'Cripper' was soon followed by the Singer tricycle produced in 1888 which, while similar in layout to the Humber, had slightly smaller rear wheels and a larger front wheel with a lower saddle and a seemingly more relaxed driving position.

In the tandem machines, various manufacturers experimented with ideas. One of these was A. Wilson who fitted a 'Rover' safety with a front seat and added a 'Kangaroo' drive to the front wheel. Of how the machine performed there is no record but it must have suffered from having two men pedalling at different paces as the earlier Starley tricycle had done.

The idea of a simple tandem, 'one behind the other' was later taken to ridiculous lengths and manufacturers offered machines that took four, six, eight and even sixteen riders. Singers, however, went one better and produced their Military machine, a couple of tandems fixed together with crossbars which was capable of carrying a large number of men. During the Boer War (1899–1902), a machine of this type was built which carried a large number of fully armed men with special wheels. The machine was constructed so that the two separate frames fixed together and corresponded with the gauge of the railway in South Africa and with its special tyre-less wheels (more like train wheels) was designed to be used on the railway lines. Although the machine featured in *With the Flag to Pretoria* – a Harmsworth publication of the period with earnest-looking moustached soldiers simulating riding – little use was made of this 'monster'. Although this side by side tandem was a large machine one of the biggest single frame tandems was the machine designed for fourteen men, over 30 feet long and dubbed the 'Quatrodecimalopede'!

The tricycle and the other multi-wheeled machines, however, began to lose their popularity in the late 1890's when the acceptance of the safety and its improved performance and sturdiness made cycling possible for all, ladies, gentlemen, young and old.

Although the tricycle declined in popularity during the 1890's with the introduction and general acceptance of the safety bicycle, there were still those who clung to that form of machine. In the main it was commercial people who found the tricycle (the machines had by this time become obsolete) could be adapted to become a delivery vehicle. In the 1890's the Post Office had adopted tricycles for use in country areas to enable more efficient letter and parcel delivery but by the turn of the century the Post Office had bowed to progress and had used safety bicycles for their services. Although the military had adopted the bicycle during the 1880's, in the volunteer movement, they never officially adopted the tricycle but a number of manufacturers and designers contrived to produce machines which mounted machine-guns of various sorts and even on one occasion a field gun on a tricycle carriage which on paper looked good but was a folly. Another 'dreamer' produced a tricycle with an armoured shield which was some 15 feet wide and was designed to protect the men who advanced behind the 'contraption'. Another inventor F. R. Simms, also produced a military machine in 1899. His was a quadricycle named the 'Motor Scout' which had a Maxim machine-gun mounted behind a shield at the front and the intrepid rider controlled the machine with his left hand while firing with his right. While the machine was never adopted Simms was not to be deterred and went on to design and have built the first armoured car powered by an internal combustion engine in 1902.

The tricycle, unlike the quadricycle never entirely disappeared from the cycling scene and although its popularity waned it had a small if faithful following. For children it was and still is the ideal machine and modern bicycles for smaller children have stabilizing wheels while for the younger ones the tricycle with direct front pedals drive has never been bettered.

Although the safety managed to oust the tricycle in popularity, it never quite managed to kill it and it still continued, and continues today as a sturdy, well balanced, reliable machine and with children, as various plates show, still the only machine for the very young.

By the turn of the century, the tricycle had attained its ultimate level, the wheels being equal in size and any improvements made to it ran side by side with the safety, although at the beginning of the twentieth century, some manufacturers both in Britain and abroad still manufactured slightly unorthodox machines, and marketed such machines as the sociable tricycle. This machine (see Plate 80) was essentially two back halves of safety machines, one with crossbar for the gentleman and one with dropped frame for the lady fitted together with differential drive with a single front wheel. Although both riders had handlebars it was the gentleman who was in charge of steering and braking, but the lady was expected to contribute to the pedalling!

Although the tricycle had a large commercial following and was used for deliveries by tradesmen as well as the Post Office, by the turn of the century, the safety with special arrangements for carrying goods and parcels was the more accepted machine.

The safety had finally triumphed over other forms of machine as being the most reliable, easiest to ride and maintain and within the reach of most, if not all.

4

The Safety Bicycle to 1900

As with other inventions, the 'safety' bicycle did not just happen but evolved over a number of years with various manufacturers and designers contributing to the advancement. As we have seen in the last chapter, the dwarf ordinaries were a step in the direction of a safety bicycle but they were still designed with propulsion coming from action on the front wheel. The first machine using the rear wheel drive by transmission of power from the pedals by a strap, as we have seen, was thought of in 1869 by Frederick Shearing, but the first inventor or designer of a machine that was feasible and had a wheel driven by a chain was Rousseau of Marseille in 1877. Rousseau produced a machine with chain drive to the front wheel while in the following year, Thomas Shergold of Gloucester produced a chain-driven machine with drive to the rear wheel. The Shergold machine (now in the Science Museum, South Kensington, London) was a crude affair when compared with the factory produced ordinaries and dwarf ordinaries but it did embody features that would find their place in the later 'safety' bicycles. Although the steering was rather complex, both wheels were of the same size, the saddle was placed over the centre of the rear wheel and two forks from the frame held a cogged wheel to which was attached cranks and pedals. This larger cogged wheel was connected to a smaller cogged wheel (thus providing suitable gearing) which was the centre of the rear wheel. So by pedalling the power was transmitted, geared up, to the rear wheel.

In the same year another chain-driven machine reached the market. This was the 'Kangaroo', a joint venture between William Hillman, W. H. Herbert and G. B. Cooper. The machine was essentially a dwarf ordinary but instead of the levers that had been previously used on other machines of this type, chains were used. The saddle was placed well back, the size of wheel reduced and the pedals lowered. To obtain the drive necessary the pedals and cranks were fitted to small cogged wheels fitted to the fork extensions and these were connected by chain to a smaller cogged wheel in the centre of the wheel. Because there were two pedals, there were two sets of wheels and chains. The machine enjoyed immense popularity for two years until the true 'safety' appeared rendering all other machines obsolete.

H. W. Lawson, whom we have seen from the previous chapter produced a machine in 1876 with a larger rear wheel than front perfected his ideas and patented a most advanced machine in 1879. Lawson who was the manager of the Tangent and Coventry Tricycle Company named his machine the 'bicyclette'. The 'bicyclette' was a revolution in design. It still however, was influenced by the ordinaries having a larger front wheel and a smaller rear one but the frame ran in a straight line from the forks holding the front wheel to the rear wheel hub. An almost vertical bar about midway held the saddle with suitable if somewhat crude adjustment for height on the upper part. A cogged wheel was connected to a small cogged wheel on the lower part, fitted to the right rear hub by a continuous small link chain. The thoughtful designer had also fitted a rear mud guard to the machine and a rear wheel brake. The steering was not however direct. To enable the rider to drive in comfort, the handlebars were set at a convenient position on the frame and connected with an arm to the top of the front fork.

When first publicly exhibited in 1880 it aroused a great deal of interest, many who saw the machine either at a show or in the window of a Coventry bicycle agent remarking on its unusual form. However, the *Cyclist* for 21 April 1880 concluded that '... its ungainly appearance is more than compensated for by its absolute and certain safety ... Mr Lawson late of Brighton, but now manager of the Tangent and Coventry Tricycle Co., habitually rides it in preference to his ordinary machine ...' However Lawson did not immediately capitalize on his novel and improved design, possibly not realizing what a breakthrough he had made or put off by the comments about its appearance. Later in the early 1880's he approached the Birmingham Small Arms Co. (B.S.A.) to undertake the manufacture of his machine but by this date even his advanced machine was obsolete, because of other developments.

B.S.A. had entered the cycle field in 1880, to maintain their work force because of decline in small arms, producing the Otto Dicycle patented by E.C.T. Otto between 1879 and 1881. This curious machine had two large wheels side by side with a space in the centre and connected with an axle and frame to which the saddle was fitted, positioned slightly behind the axle pedals. Cranks were fitted to driving wheels on the frame extension and connected to another set of wheels at the hub of the large road wheels by a steel belt. B.S.A. had high hopes of this machine scooping the market, but they made about a thousand before abandoning it. It did, however, attract some of the cycling fraternity who proudly called themselves Ottoists.

During this and earlier periods, the bicycle was constantly menaced by the popularity of the tricycle (see Chapter III) but it was the developments made during the 1880's which would finally establish the supremacy of the bicycle. In 1884 B.S.A. had taken out a patent (15342) for a safety bicycle although they were unable to call it that as Lawson had previously registered the name 'Safety'. This machine, one of the first of many rudimentary type safety bicycles to appear in the 1880's was because of the cost factor made wherever possible from tricycle parts which B.S.A. manufactured as well as the Otto Dicycle, and rifle clearing rods of which many tens of thousands were in store. The machine was curious in shape, perhaps more so than Lawson's 'bicyclette' but unlike that machine, the B.S.A. bicycle had a larger rear wheel and a small front wheel suitably equipped with foot rests so the rider could take his feet off and coast, there being no 'free wheel' on the machine. The saddle was mounted just in front of the rear wheel fitted thoughtfully with a mud guard and the handlebars just in front, linked with the rifle clearing rods to an arm that turned the front wheel. Fitted to the lower part of the frame was the usual cogged wheel over which a chain passed to the smaller cogged wheel fitted to the back wheel.

In the same year, however, Humber and Co. produced their own version of the safety bicycle, which was the first to reduce the influence of the ordinary although the designer could not shake himself free of having one large and one small wheel. The frame consisted of a single almost upright column at the front with, at the top part, a bar joined which ran back, holding the saddle above the rear wheel then sloped down in two forks to hold the rear wheel and another bar from the bottom of the front column which held the cogged driving wheel and connected again with two forks to the rear wheel hub. The steering was, on this machine, direct, that is there was no system of levers and links. The height of both saddle and handlebars was adjustable. The manufacturers, however, still thought it necessary to provide a mounting step fitted to the rear wheel hub.

Another machine produced in the same year was manufactured by J. McCammon, his machine being essentially a ladies' model. The machine had once again a larger rear wheel and a smaller front one and direct steering. The front steering column with forks for the wheel was a separate item joined to the main frame with hinged links (the Humber machine had a slightly different arrangement) while the main frame curved from the lower part of the steering column down to the position where the pedals and cogged wheel were fitted and then up and over the fore part of the rear wheel ending in two descending forks. The saddle was mounted on the rising rear part of the frame and was suitably sprung with coiled springs and adjustable.

Another, but perhaps the most famous safety was produced by John Kemp Starley in the same year. His first machine had very little more to offer than the B.S.A machine and looked remarkably like it. The original machine had a larger front wheel and a smaller rear one and a frame which dipped down in similar fashion to the ordinary frame to the pedals and cogged driving wheel with forks at the front and at the rear. The top part of the frame included the indirect steering links and rods, bar for the adjustable saddle and two rear forks to the hub for support. However, the following year at the suggestion of Stephen Golder, a Coventry pressman and experienced cyclist, Starley employed direct steering while still retaining the basic shape of the earlier model without of course the rod indirect steering. Still not entirely satisfied with his efforts, Starley produced yet another model in 1885 and this time the true 'safety' was born.

To gain acceptance by the public of the machine and to establish it, Starley needed an endurance feat and hoping to snatch the market from the still popular dwarf ordinaries hired racing cyclists and proceeded to establish records. In September 1885, he succeeded in his quest when one of his riders, George Smith, rode 100 miles in 7 hours 5 minutes and 16 seconds. Not resting on his laurels Starley produced an even better safety, the third of the 'Rover' series. This, like the second model had indirect steering but an improved frame. In place of the thin connecting bar between front steering column and rear forks he made a stronger slightly downdrooping crossbar, strengthened the front and rear forks and simplified the method of mounting the saddle.

While Starley may well have been pleased with his design and his record, it was a short-lived win for less than a month later William Hillman's rider completed the 100 miles in 6 hours 39 minutes and 5 seconds on a 'Premier' safety which he brought out in the same year.

Other manufacturers started to introduce their safety machines at this time to catch on to the growing cycle boom. Mass production meant that machines now sold even cheaper than before while even the very poor could content themselves with discarded ordinaries at knock-down prices. Amongst the machines available at this time was the 'Ivel' produced in 1886 by Dan Albourne, the landlord of the Olney Arms on the Great North Road, who besides pulling pints for his customers was a cyclist, a record breaker and manufacturer. His machine had broken the 50 mile record in the year it was introduced by covering the course in 2 hours 4 minutes and 45 seconds and later achieved 295 miles in 24 hours. The 'Ivel' like the McCammon machine had a drop frame and no crossbar but like others had a larger front wheel and a smaller rear one.

Another significant machine that appeared at this time was the 'Whippet' manufactured by Lindley and Biggs who introduced their machine on to the market in 1885. Because of the poor but improving conditions of the roads – although some especially in and around cities had improved – their design incorporated an elementary form of shock absorber. This idea was not new however as some form of elementary springing had been used before, one example being the tricycle 'Monarch' estate car made in the 1880's. (See Chapter III and Plate 43.) But unfortunately, as we shall see, the 'Whippet' which could have claimed a large portion of the market came at an unfortunate time. The 'Whippet' was a safety bicycle with tube frame, direct steering and chain drive but its uniqueness lay in the construction of the frame. The frame of the machine was sprung, but the position of the saddle, handlebars and pedals was not altered as they were constructed on a separate and rigid frame. The machine employed flexible joints and springs, a coiled one stretching from the front driving and cogged wheel to the crossframe and a link arm between the upright holding the saddle and the lower crossframe. The important event that overtook and rendered this machine out of date was the introduction of the pneumatic tyre.

Solid rubber tyres had been introduced previously for bicycles to cushion some of the harsh impact caused by road surfaces and later the cushion rubber tyre was introduced, to try and give the cyclist a smoother ride. All these tyres were bonded on to the rim of the wheel in various ways and although they were an improvement on the iron-shod wheels and solid leather or rubber, were far from perfect. The first pneumatic tyre, or air-filled tyre had been invented by R. W. Thomason in his patent 10990 of 1845 but this far-sighted inventor had, presumably because of the almost non-existence of any form of cycle designed his tyre for coaches, bath chairs, rocking chairs and railway carriages but in 1888 John Boyd Dunlop, a Scot and veterinary surgeon by profession sought a way to make his son's tricycle easier and more comfortable to ride, so the story goes. He fitted an air-filled tube to a wooden disc which he made and covered in canvas; nailing the covering to the wood wheel; then rolling it as well as a plain wood disc, he found that the one with his tyre went farther than the other. His next move was to fit his son's tricycle with the tyre he had 'invented'. In 1889, Dunlop applied for and was granted a patent No 4116 for an air-filled tube with outer covering, the outer cover being secured to the wheel by cement and binding.

Dunlop soon formed a company to manufacture the tyre he had perfected and unlike the previous inventor channelled all his thoughts towards the booming cycle industry. His early tyres had an inflated inner tube with a cemented outer cover but with the prevalent road conditions this could hardly have been satisfactory for within a few years pneumatic tyres appeared on the market that could be detached easily from the rim of the wheel to enable replacement to be made or a puncture to be repaired. Various inventors tried their hand at a suitable solution such as the wired-on type patented by C. K. Welch and a tyre with a wedge or beaded edge patented by W. Bartlett, but it was not until the 1890's that both the Dunlop Rubber Company Ltd and the brothers André and Edouard Michelin of France perfected better methods of attaching and detaching tyres to effect repairs. In spite of the advent of this new tyre which revolutionized cycle travel, inventors still continued with their work and in 1892 a certain Mr Lungren filed a patent in Washington D.C. for a tubeless tyre. While some thought this a step backwards those careful enough to read the specifications would have found that the tyre had two soft rubber rings on which the tyre beads were seated and that the outer tyre was separate from the inflated inner one.

Other patents on this principle were taken out during the 1890's in America but Britain and Europe clung to the Dunlop and Michelin product, although various ingenious inventors tempted the growing number of cyclists and manufacturers with their products. The Preston–Davies tyre was held to the rim by a series of staples which corresponded with wires or loops in the outer casing while the Leyland Pneumatic tyre had studs fitted to the tyre which neatly clipped into the corresponding holes in the rim of the wheel. Another ingenious invention was the Hook tyre which was fitted with a series of hooks which clipped well over the rim

64

and on to the spokes of the wheel. Another inventive creation was the Swindley-Manhole tyre which had a cemented-on tyre to the wheel but had a trapdoor in the rim of the wheel through which the inner tube could be pulled out for repair and then replaced. However, one ingenious inventor patented the Wright Protector which was a tyre fitted on the inside with metal scales, fitted lobster tail fashion. This ingenious device – the creator declared – rendered punctures impossible but this and other highly impractical tyres soon disappeared from the market leaving the now conventional inflatable tyres of Dunlop and Michelin.

While the tyres had been progressing so had the machines to which they were fitted. In the 1880's various designers had tried to introduce variable gears on the machine rather than the set gear, although this could be varied on custom-made machines when ordered. In 1887 the Sparkbook machine boasted two-speed gears but this involved two driving chains and was deemed impractical and it was only in the 1890's despite efforts of others, many of them inventive and sound in design but impractical in use that a suitable gearing hub was invented or at least developed.

Meanwhile there had been more advances in the design of the bicycle itself, although there were as always the diehards who continued to ride their ordinaries come what may, while manufacturers – there were few – refused to accept the chain-driven machine and still produced their own designs. One prime example was the Crypto 'geared Facile' reminiscent of the ordinary which was produced in 1888 still with lever pedals to drive the larger front wheel. Crypto stuck out to the last with their machines producing in 1894 – when the safety was well and truly established – a Bantam Crypto still with larger front wheel and with gearing in the front hub with front wheel cranks and pedals. Refusing to accept defeat they produced in 1896 an improved version, this time with wheels the same size but still with the geared front hub cranks and pedals. As it turned out, this was the last of the front-wheel drive bicycles, for by this time, many improvements in design and performance had firmly established the safety as the *only* machine with two wheels.

By the end of the 1880's however, in spite of a few individualists as there were and always are in many fields, the safety was firmly established, together with the diamond frame developed by Humber. Other companies adopted this method of frame construction which was not only easier for mass production but was an added advantage to cycle design. The established firms keeping up with the times produced their safety machines but such was the boom that companies who were unconnected with the cycle industry quickly formulated designs and plans to introduce machines of their own. At this period, smaller manufacturers could buy component parts from the larger companies and still produce some variant on standard design, but it was only the ability to purchase such frames, gears, etc. that enabled the independent maker of a small number of specialized machines to be competitive.

The cycle boom which occurred in the 1890's attracted a large number of outside manufacturers who were engaged in a variety of engineering and light engineering businesses. The industrial centres like Birmingham and London as well as others were affected as manufacturers strove to turn out not only their own machines but the components that an increasing number of small and large firms required. Companies like Armstrong of Elswick, better known as 'cannon Kings', turned to cycles dubbing their product the Elswick while other manufacturers of armaments (we have already seen B.S.A. as a front runner in the safety cycle business) such as Wilkinson Sword Company – more renowned for their swords and bayonets – and large government contractors added cycles to their list or products. Whitworth, another armament king, went into partnership to produce bicycles. The 'Pall Mall' cycle was a custom-built machine composed mainly of B.S.A. parts but with an extraordinary attention to detail and finish. Besides building machines from commercial parts these 'manufacturers' on occasion contributed to the development of the cycle, even if some of their ideas and patents were strange to say the least.

Wilkinsons with their 'Pall Mall' cycle so named after the illustrious street in which stood their head office and which once housed the War Office – gunmakers, sword cutlers and tailors – were one of the manufacturers to modify the 'safety' and introduce a shaft-driven machine to replace the now accepted chain drive. The company claimed that the shaft was not only made from 'sword steel' but was a forged sword blade, but the idea of shaft drive never caught on and it was abandoned. Others too had tried shaft drive as far back as 1882 in Britain and the U.S.A. and the famous arms manufacturers of Liège in Belgium F.N. (Fabrique Nationale) had also introduced machines with a shaft drive. Although most of the shaft-driven machines boasted a gearing with turning rod shaft with internally toothed pedal wheel it was only the Wilkinson Sword Company which announced their sword blade shaft. Another shaft-driven machine was manufactured in Germany and called the Durkopp after the manufacturers Durkoppwerk A.G. or Reinckendorf. Like the other shaft-driven machines it never caught on with the public and soon faded.

None of these novelty inventions, however, deterred the public from buying the safety bicycle which through the various manufacturers had established a firm hold on the market. With the standardization of the safety design even if manufacturers had their own pet ideas, they all conformed to the diamond frame principle with makers having added refinements in saddle, brakes, etc.

This vast increase in the cycle trade and the lowering of prices by mass production by the mid-1890's caused innumerable problems to various concerns which employed labour usually on a piecework basis either in their own factories or in their homes. This was perhaps felt more acutely in

Birmingham where pieceworking and outworkers were the mainstay of diverse industries. Frederick Mole of the sword and bayonet contractors, Robert Mole and Son, wrote to J. Wilkinson-Latham (the author's grandfather) of Wilkinson's concerning a sword contract in 1896 that he could not complete, as many of his workers had been '... induced to go to bycycle [sic] work ...' Mole, unlike Wilkinson, had not entered the cycle trade and his business suffered because his outworkers could earn more in this booming industry.

Of the safety bicycles that were made at the beginning of the 1890's there were four varieties; those made as a mass produced item by an established company, those assembled by a company with their own refinements, those locally made from manufactured components and the 'de luxe' machines, custom built without regard to cost.

While the larger companies produced machines for the mass market there were the smaller firms which designed and produced bicycles for a smaller, richer and more specialist market. The first to cater for this market was the Dursley Pedersen, a scientifically designed machine constructed by Lister and Co. of Dursley after the design of a Danish inventor Mikael Pedersen. Because of the arrangement of the tubes of the frame on the cantilever principle, the components of the frame could be thinner and smaller than the conventional safety machine. One of the main features of the machine was the strange hammock saddle made of silk cord suspended between the seat pillar and the steering head. The main advantage was that it could be adjusted for tightness or looseness and as the catalogue stated '... this saddle adjusts itself to every movement of the body, and allows perfect freedom for those muscles which cycling brings into play'. Other specialized machines did not, however, appear until after 1900 and are dealt with in Chapter VI.

The cycling boom of the first 6 years of the 1890's was, however, destined for a slump and many of the companies went bankrupt because of over-capitalization but others such as Raleigh held on and profited from an upsurge in the cycle industry that came in the early years of the new century. It was during the so-called slump in the industry that many improvements were made to the safety machine. The main improvements were to do with the drive of the machine, gearing and perhaps most significant of all the free wheel. No longer would machines have to be equipped with foot-rests when travelling downhill so that the cyclist could remove his feet from the fast-revolving pedals.

However, there were certain drawbacks to being a cycle manufacturer and an article in *The West Middlesex Advertiser* for Friday 25 September 1896, the first in a series entitled 'Chelsea Industries' remarked that 'the cycle trade in England is somewhat hampered by the stringency of the patent monopolies and also by the prejudices of English cyclists as regards the particular tyres'.

By the 1890's the large firms had established their reputation and names such as Raleigh, B.S.A., Humber, Rudge-Whitworth, Triumph, Swift, Baylis and Thomas and of course Rover were forefront in the production of commercial machines. In 1895, these firms together with the other smaller makers produced, as *The Cycle* reported, some 800,000 bicycles. Cycling was a booming pastime during the early 1890's and popular songs of the music halls mirrored the passion for the safety bicycle with all its refinements.

The chorus of one such song went as follows:

'Sally rode a Raleigh, and I journeyed on a Rudge,
I said I'd stick to Sally, and she said she'd never budge.
But Mohawks came and Singers came, and Rovers
    without number,
And one fine day, she rode away with a beast on a
    Beeston Humber.'

Another contemporary song demonstrating the joy of social cycling now that ladies could use the safety had a chorus that went as follows:

'Rhoda rode a roadster on the road to Ryde,
I rode a roadster on the road by Rhoda's side,
When next I ride to Ryde with Rhoda she will be my
    bride,
Oh! Bless the day that Rhoda rode a roadster.'

While it was a boom that pervaded all levels of society, the aristocracy of all countries and even royalty and members of society felt bound to be seen on their machines. In 1897 for example, the Touring Club de France listed a great number of foreign honorary members including the King of the Belgians, the Prince of Wales, Prince Nicholas of Greece, the Grand-Duke Sergei Michailovich, and other European crowned heads.

The fringe firms which made cycles from parts supplied by others with perhaps one or two refinements of their own were supplied by companies such as Abingdon-Ecco but perhaps the largest amount of components came from B.S.A.

During the 1880's a number of gears had appeared on the market one of which was the Sparkbrook which employed two driving chains introduced in 1887 but perhaps the most important was the three-speed Jay gearing of 1883 from which modern gearing evolved. S. J. Collier patented a two-speed gear in 1889 but the first commercially viable gearing was patented by W. Reilly in 1896. Other inventors too brought out their gearing systems, two, three and even four speed, many of which were used to a limited scale on commercial machines.

By the end of the decade cycling, although in the doldrums, still attracted some buyers although not to the extent of the early years of the decade. Cycle shows were still held and manufacturers and those that 'assembled' machines continued to try and woo the public. In the *Daily Mail* for 20 November 1899 the front page, in spite of the Boer War being in progress, carried a large number of advertisements for the cycle trade. Dunlop tyres took a large space reminding potential clients to come and visit them at the National Cycle Show at Crystal Palace, as did the New Rapid Cycle Co. Ltd of Birmingham, which claimed to be the pioneers of long cranks and high gears. The North Rubber Tyre Co., a rival of Dunlop were also there. The Wilkinson Sword Company urged cyclists to see their free wheel and back pedalling rim brake while the Coventry Eagle Cycle Co. advertised their free wheels and back pedalling brakes (rim and band). This rear wheel brake worked by back pedalling which engaged a small clutch on the rear wheel. There were advertisements for self-sealing air tubes for pneumatic tyres, the Folshill Cycle Co. with their ball-bearing free wheel, the Bricknell auxiliary hand gear, and the Esmond cycle saddle 'guaranteed to prevent all saddle discomforts.'

The same paper carried advertisements for the rival Stanley Show which besides having stands had cycle entertainment such as Trick Riding Entertainment by the Villion Troupe and was patronized by Rudge-Whitworth, the Aceatene (chainless) Cycle with free wheel and back pedalling brake, the Hepworth cycle with quick detachable hubs, the Wapshare detachable tyre, the Abingdon cycle with back pedalling brake and free wheel, but perhaps the most ominous sign of the time was the presence of the Motor Manufacturing Co. Ltd, which were exhibiting the finest selection of motor cars and motorcycles.

Another advertisement in the same column announced the sale of some 300 cycles including Humbers at the Vulcan Auction Mart in Ludgate Hill, London, machines discarded by those in society for whom the craze had ceased. The society boom in 1895 and the following year had been a phenomenon in London and other major cities. Rotten Row in London's Hyde Park usually reserved for the more elegant pursuit of horse-riding had, during the weekends, been filled with cyclists riding up and down, being seen, meeting friends and generally indulging in a social pastime.

One notable and important aspect of this cavorting was

71

that amongst the many male cyclists there were a great many female cyclists for whom the safety machine had meant a great deal. With the new designs, manufacturers started to make special models exclusively for the lady rider. These machines were fitted with guards to the chain and nets over the back wheel to avoid any nasty accidents of having the long dresses becoming entangled with the spokes or chains.

Women cyclists had in the years before, started their encroachment on this male-dominated hobby but the design of the machines gave them little chance of competing. The early machines like the Micheaux had given some the chance to ride but with the advent of the ordinary, except for an effort by James Starley and a few others to build a lady-like side-saddle machine which was almost impossible to manoeuvre, lady cyclists had to be content with the more sedate tricycles or 'sociables' where they were accompanied by a male companion.

The safety, however, gave ladies a chance to ride solo once more. While some of these ladies still clung to their long dresses suitably protected from being snagged with the mechanics of the machine, others appeared in 'rational' dress which included plus-fours, bloomers, and leggings, etc. These ladies were soon nicknamed 'Scortchers' and were to be seen in Hyde Park, St James's Park, Battersea Park and elsewhere pursuing their hobby. The majority of these ladies availed themselves of the safetys especially designed for the female sex without the customary crossbar and an additional lower strengthening bar to the frame. Decency, it seems, was outraged in 1893 when Miss Tessie Reynolds of Brighton rode a machine from Brighton to London and back wearing 'rational' dress, in company with some young men from Brighton. She completed 120 miles in $8\frac{1}{2}$ hours and although widely congratulated by women there was a different reaction amongst the men. The reaction was not because of 'rational' dress, not perhaps that she cycled together with young men but that she actually rode on a machine made for men!

Public opinion had by the 1890's accepted 'rational' dress and even females riding cycles, although some eminent medical men had been at pains to point out, without medical foundation, that the riding of machines of this nature was injurious to the female form and could, as *Cycling* pointed out in an issue of 7 October 1893, distort the pelvis '... with perhaps, in after life, resulting distress'. However, two years later this magazine and others had completely changed their minds and an outing on a bicycle was advocated for health against the cramped and restricted life of women at the time. The change in heart had perhaps been brought about by the Rational Society, which as early as the late 1880's had campaigned for women and bicycles. While rational dress might be accepted in London but only just and by a minority in Paris it was *de rigueur* and considered the height of fashion. Because of this move of emancipation, cycle manufacturers actively encouraged the ladies to ride their machines and strove to provide suitable models for 'rational' and conventional dress.

It was not, however, until the opening years of the twentieth century that female cycling was fully accepted and what had been a hobby for some became a cheap and useful mode of transport for all. By this time, those who had seen cycles, tricycles, etc. as a social fad had progressed to the even newer social fad of the motor car.

Record breaking was still foremost in the minds of the manufacturers, and in 1892, the Land's End to John o' Groats ride had been accomplished in 3 days, 23 hours and 55 minutes which was reduced by some 17 hours in 1894. By 1898 with the improved safety cycles, gearing, etc. the 100 mile record stood at 4 hours 16 minutes and 35 seconds. Record-making journeys were also useful to manufacturers and the sponsored riders (more than one maker of cycles and cycle items were involved) benefited from these feats of endurance. Robert Jefferson, an author who wrote about his mammoth cycle adventures completed a journey to Moscow and back covering 4,281 miles in 49 days on a machine he had especially stripped of superfluous weight for this journey. Those that benefited with advertising from this escapade were Dunlop with their tyres, Wood with their wire saddle, Grose's gearcase, Starley with his Rover frame and Perry who supplied the chains and the Signal Fork Cyclometer which measured the mileage.

By the turn of the century, the free wheel was a standard item of the safety bicycle and gears an essential, and the public could avail itself of the latest products of Singer, Elswick, Raleigh, Lindley and Biggs with their 'New Whippet' fitted with four-speed gearing or if so disposed with any other makes available including one or two shaft-driven models, which never could equal the simplicity of the firmly established safety.

With the improvements of the machine came the improvement of the various indispenable accessories which no self-respecting cyclist would be seen without. Chain cases were provided as an extra by some for ladies' machines, while various models of saddle were available with leaf or coil spring and suitably padded. Some companies went one stage further and introduced what they claimed were scientifically designed saddles. One of these was the Anatomically Perfect Hygienic saddle of 1895 which was a form-fitting saddle suitable for all. Rim brakes had been fitted to most machines by the late 1890's and pedals were more suitably made from rubber. Chains had also advanced during this period from crudely made ones to the roller-chain design by J. Slater and perfected by H. Reynolds by the turn of the century. H. Carter, another inventor designed the case which enclosed the chain, protecting it from dust, dirt and grit from road surfaces and at the same time providing a sump-like arrangement which meant continuous lubrication. An advance had also been made with cycle lamps from the early acetylene ones of the 1880's, which continued for some time before Joseph Lucas produced his 'King of the Road' and 'Silver King' selection of lamps. It was not, however, until 1910 that acetylene and oil-burning lamps were slowly ousted by the Bowden cycle dynamo, although the Lucas acetylene lamp was still being sold in 1940!

In 1888 when it was declared by statute that the bicycle was a carriage, it became obligatory for all cyclists to have a bell fitted to their machines, although many fitted horns or other warning devices. The cycle clubs usually had a bugler in their midst to announce their arrival or to give warning to other road users. By the turn of the century these eccentricities had passed away and most machines were fitted with a simple bell on the handlebars.

5

The Bicycle as a War Horse 1875–1945

The first use of the bicycle by any military forces was by the Italian army in 1875. During the annual manoeuvres a number of cyclists with their machines were used as despatch riders between commander and troops 'in the field'. It seems to have been a success and was retained in the Italian army for some years. It was not however, until over 10 years later that other European countries followed this lead. In Britain, bicycles even if not with the blessing of the authorities were used in 1885 but three years prior to this in 1882 it had already been suggested in the press that a volunteer corps of cyclists should be formed. The main drawback was not the authorities in this case but the very machine itself which was thought to be entirely unsuited to this form of work and one cannot be surprised at this attitude if one considers the sight of soldiers mounted on ordinaries!

With the coming of the Safety bicycle (see Chapter IV) mounting troops on bicycles became a practical proposition.

The first use in Britain was at the Easter manoeuvres in 1885 when Major Bloomfield, the adjutant of the 1st Sussex Rifle Volunteers, mounted his men on bicycles and issued them with revolvers hastily borrowed from the local coast-guard. A contemporary account in the *Brighton Herald* (4 April 1885) stated that

> 'The regiment went out equipped more completely than ever before. Not only were there a signalling party and an ambulance party (thus fulfilling a wish expressed by the Colonel after the Portsmouth Review), but it was also accompanied by a startling novelty in military affairs, in the shape of a party of bicyclists, for scouting purposes. There were six in all, namely, Corporal A. Smith (B Company), Lance-Corporal Crone (B), Private Russell (B), Private Baskett (C), Private Cooper (F) and Private Boxall (F). They were armed with revolvers, and did good service in their special work, though, as the fortune of war would have it, three of them fell into the hands of the enemy.'

However, it was not until the introduction of the safety bicycle that these mounted troops were taken seriously. The impetus was given by a Colonel A. Saville who was then the instructor of Tactics at the Staff College at Camberley. In 1887, he paraded the first military cyclists at Canterbury mounted on a variety of machines. It seems however, that this early demonstration had the desired effect because in the same year, Major Edge of the Royal Marines was given permission by the Lords of the Admiralty to form a corps of volunteer military cyclists and it was even thought that this sort of machine would be eminently suitable for the ship-borne marine when landed ashore for duty. A committee was set up to inquire into the why's and wherefores and the advantages of 'mounting' marines on cycles. In its short sitting it produced a report that was favourably considered by the authorities and in the following year there was formed the 26th Middlesex (Cyclist) Volunteer Rifle Corps, with Colonel Saville, late of the Staff College as its commanding officer. Because of the diversity of machines, the corps was divided into separate troops, one with safeties, one with ordinaries and one with tricycles totalling in all 121 of all ranks. This establishment was soon increased and the corps proudly boasted having over 360 'mounted' members. This unprecedented step in military thinking had repercussions throughout the volunteer movement but the Regular army generally viewed the replacement of the horse for cycle in cavalry troops and any change in the traditional role of the foot soldier in the rifles and infantry with distaste and disdain. By the first decade of the twentieth century, more cyclists sections were formed but again only in the volunteer or as they were to be known in 1908 the Territorial Force, and it was not until 1915 when a Royal Warrant authorized the formation of the Army Cyclist Corps that the Regular army was forced to accept these inevitabilities.

The Royal Engineers, like the Royal Artillery which took their professions seriously – too seriously was the considered opinion of cavalry and infantry officers – saw the possibility of the bicycle and experimented with it to tow small trailers with tools for engineering works and for telegraph cable laying, but they were only experiments.

Other countries viewed the possibility of the bicycle with a less-biased eye and these included, apart from the European countries such as Belgium, France and Austria as well as Italy, the United States. At the North-Western Military Academy, Wisconsin, a small section of sixteen cyclists was formed which were equipped with rifle clips and straps to carry equipment and other necessaries. This small group seems to have been very proficient because they are recorded as having scaled, with their overloaded machines, a 16 foot high wall in 3 minutes taking all their equipment with them without any mishap. The American Ordnance seemed to have been highly impressed with this demonstration of the usefulness of the bicycle and ordered the Pope Manufacturing Company (see Chapter III) to design a suitable machine on which to mount a machine-gun.

In Belgium, because of the terrain, cycles were obviously more advantageous to troops and the Government decided on the great advantage of possessing these machines when a general mobilization took place. In Austria and France the military authorities had authorized the development of a suitable machine for military purposes. The Austrians in 1896 had developed a machine that folded in half and was able to be carried knapsack fashion on the back of the soldier and France followed suit in 1898. Until now, however, although the bicycle had been tried by a number of countries it had not performed in wartime conditions. Others apart from the military had employed the bicycle in wartime conditions and these included the famous war correspondent and artist of the *Graphic*, the bearded Frederick Villiers. A great self-advertiser and raconteur (mainly about himself) Villiers was the first man to use the cycle on campaign and went to great lengths to inform the world of his 'first'. The first recorded use of the bicycle as a mode of transport for the war correspondent was during the Greco–Turkish War (1897) when a Greek newspaperman used the bicycle throughout the war, and later when his memoirs were published the sale of bicycles in Athens increased greatly! Villiers arrived in Cairo for the Omdurman campaign with his 'dark green roadster' a safety, and one of many offered at this time. After the battle, Villiers disappeared in search of news and it was noted by Bennet Burleigh, the famed correspondent of the *Daily Telegraph* that his machine '... was disfigured by an honourable scar, for the top of the valve was gone, and Hassan declared that it had been carried away by a Dervish bullet'.

Villier's machine was described as being '... of a dull green tint' and the 'lugubrious-looking bicycle bore the battle and breeze wonderfully well, and the maker ought to secure a splendid advertisement out of it; for the tyres which pass unpunctured through the terrors of the mimosa scrub, and refrain from bursting under the rays of a Sudan sun in August, may fairly be recommended for "strong roadster" work in the country lanes of England'.

The cycle industry was not, however, slow to see the possibilities of a machine for the ubiquitous war correspondent and in the *Regiment* in October 1896 a machine was described 'calculated to stand the wear and tear of rough riding across country. Upon the handlebar is to be attached a typewriter, on which the operator will record all his impressions of the battle surging around him ...' War correspondents, however, fought shy of this 'devilish machine' and continued to use the safety for transport where the terrain permitted.

To return to military machines, the Boer War which broke out 'at tea time' as *The Times* humorously put it in its edition of 11 October 1899, saw the first consistent use of the bicycle in warfare. A number of the cyclists were equipped with the folding Dursley-Pedersen machine which was light and admirable for the purpose but others – the majority – were equipped with solid frame safety machines.

It was the Boer War which was to prove the value of the cycle but in a limited way. Terrain had always to be considered for, while the cycle might be quite easy to operate, easy to maintain and required no fodder, the horse over broken ground and hilly terrain was superior. However, during the Boer War cyclists did go to South Africa where the veldt was a most suitable type of terrain on which to ride. According to René Bull, war artist and correspondent for the *Black and White* magazine, 'the bicycle had proved itself very serviceable during the present war. The rider is less conscious than he would be on a horse, though of course he has to risk punctures and gears going out of order.' Cyclist scouts were employed in a number of areas, although crossing drifts was a little complicated on these machines. In *With the Flag to*

Pretoria, a Harmsworth part work on the Boer War, the author H. W. Wilson stated that 'in a land where the mortality amongst horses was so great, the ever-ready cycle has been of great value'.

In 1901, the authorities, convinced by the success however moderate of the bicycle in South Africa allowed the Rifle Volunteer Corps with an establishment of over 600 to include a company of cyclists as scouts of not more than seventy-five men, and many of the volunteer battalions strove to raise their numbers for the honour of including a prestige cycle company. However, in 1908 with the formation of the Territorial Force (later the Territorial Army) there were a number of cyclist 'battalions' linked to regular regiments because of the organization and linking of regular militia and Volunteer forces. On 20 July 1908, however, the War Office sent a memorandum to all Territorial infantry battalions empowering them to raise a cyclist section of fifteen of all ranks. This did not of course affect the volunteers who were wholly cyclist battalions such as the 25th (County of London) Btn – formerly the 26th Middlesex Volunteers – 6th Btn the Norfolk Regt, 7th Btn the Welsh Regt, and others which included the three units that were converted prior to 1908, the 10th Btn the Royal Scots converted from the 8th Volunteer Btn, the 5th Btn East Yorkshire Regt formed from the 2nd Volunteer Btn and the Highland Cyclist Btn formed from the 5th Volunteer Btn of the Black Watch.

The machine that was almost entirely used by the cyclist was the 'B.S.A. Territorial Bicycle'. The following specifications of this sturdy machine are taken from a pre-World War I catalogue produced by the Wilkinson Sword Company who were agents for B.S.A.

FRAME Built with best selected butted steel tubing D section back forks and stays; made in the following heights: 23 in., 24 in., 25 in., 26 in. and 27 in.

81

FRONT FORK	Special taper gauge steel blades, D to round section, fitted with solid steel machined-slotted ends, which allow of the front wheel being removed without straining the fork.
WHEELS	28 in., equal, constructed with best double butted steel spokes. Westwood or Wedgewood rims highly polished and heavily nickel-plated, edges and centres enamelled and lined.
TYRES	Dunlop, Palmer or Clipper Ideal $1\frac{1}{2}$ in., with wired or beaded edges.
FITTINGS	B.S.A. throughout, light roadster pattern with 7 in. cranks.
BACK HUB	Eadie coaster.
CHAIN	B.S.A. $\frac{1}{2}$ in. pitch, tested to a strain of 2,000 lbs.
GEAR	74, or to order.
PEDALS	B.S.A. rat trap or rubber; size to order.
HANDLEBAR	B.S.A. flat or upturned pattern by 18 in. fitted with celluloid grips or a special design.
BRAKE	B.S.A. front rim brake with rolling lever, curved to suit the design of the handlebar. Solid brazed clips and with B.S.A. patent detachable shoes.
SADDLE	Brooks' B90 1, with enamelled springs.
MUDGUARDS	B.S.A. steel with forward extension and plated stays with patent detachable ends.
RIFLE CLIPS	Brooks best quality as illustrated.

BACK CARRIER	Strong serviceable carrier, specially suitable for Territorial purposes.
FINISH	Four coats of brilliant best black jet or khaki enamel on one coat of rust-proof preparation. The usual bright parts are heavily plated, and the finish is of the well-known B.S.A. high standard of quality.
	Equipped with 15 in. cellular inflator, plated clips complete with tool bag, oiler, and the necessary B.S.A. spanners to fit all nuts cones and cups.

The standard model was priced at £10, the same machine but fitted with Eadie two-speed hub and B.S.A. rolling lever brakes was £10 17s. 6d. (£10.87½p). But if the machine was fitted with the Eadie two-speed coaster and B.S.A. front rim brakes the price rose to £11 2s. 6d. (£11.22½p) but the ultimate was the machine fitted with B.S.A. three-speed hub and *two* B.S.A. rolling lever brakes priced at £11 7s. 6d. (£11.37½p).

In 1904, Lieutenant A. H. Trapman of the 26th Middlesex (Cyclist) Volunteers published a small booklet entitled *Cyclists in Action* and 2 years later the Army Council issued a manual, as they did for all new items of equipment in use. Naturally drill was regulated as well and included such useful information on saluting mounted or dismounted, riding at attention, riding at ease, grounding and stacking machines as well as the care and maintenance of the machine. 'Bicycle tyres,' stated the manual, 'should be wiped clean with a damp cloth after a march, so that all the grit, which if left might cause a puncture, may be removed.' The regulations were most particular when it came to the coastal defence role and insisted that 'All ranks of cyclist units employed in coast defence should be trained in the use of the telephone'.

Saluting while on a military machine while posing a small problem of not looking where the cyclist was going at least did not require him to remove one hand from the handlebar and salute in the conventional manner. A salute was accomplished by coming to attention on the machine and giving an 'eyes left' or 'eyes right'. This seems a somewhat dangerous manoeuvre when riding in bunched columns but few accidents are recorded.

The value of cyclists was appreciated at the outbreak of World War I and in 1915 the Army Cyclist Corps was formed and all cyclists attached or forming part of Territorial regiments were transferred to the new corps. Home defence was augmented by converting horsed yeomanry and territorial line battalions into cyclists. Some idea of the use of bicycles by the armed forces can be gleaned from the returns of issue and in 10 months of 1915, from Calais alone 12,800 bicycles were issued.

The problem of arming the cyclist was of paramount importance and although the earliest attempt mentioned above when revolvers were used was a suitable answer, cyclists soon carried long arms. To carry these, special straps and later clips were fitted to sling the weapon on the bicycle. Officers of course, carried their sword suitably strapped to the front handlebars and forks. Officers also carried a revolver on their belt.

The problem of arming the cyclist appealed to some inventors who immediately went to work. One such inventive genius produced the handlebar pepper-box six shot revolver. This ingenious gun with folding trigger was housed inside of the grip of the handlebar, being retained by a spring clip. The cyclist under attack had only to press the stud on the top of the grip with his thumb while still holding the grip and pull out the revolver whose trigger sprung down into the firing position.

The training of the cyclist was of paramount importance and in an age of unmechanized warfare he was trained to 'receive cavalry' by forming a zareba (thorn hedge constructed in square formation for protection during the Sudan campaign) of bicycles, each one placed on its side with wheels in the air. The gallant cyclists then formed a square inside with rifles at the ready. A handy tip when engaging horsed cavalry was to spin the wheels of the cycles to frighten the horses! During World War I, a Midlands manufacturer designed a protective shield for infantry mounted on the front of a bicycle. The shield suitably pierced for the muzzle of the rifle was moved forward by a soldier who slowly pedalled forward as his comrades advanced on foot behind the shield. It was never taken up by the authorities.

The cyclist was, however, taken seriously and more so by the Kaiser's intelligence department. It circulated a report to certain Naval Staff officers concerning the proposed landing sites on the coast of East Anglia which stated that 'The two agreed selected landing areas are too well guarded ... Both areas are manned by detachments of the London Cyclist Regiment, who, although only territorial soldiers, have been much remarked for their alertness and ability'. Air attacks the report continued failed to divert the troops from their vigilant watch on the coast. The British cyclists were indeed well prepared having had serious instruction from *Handbook on Military Bicycles* 1911 on what to do in case of invasion. The manual states that 'Should an enemy succeed in landing, cyclist patrols should at once establish pickets on all roads radiating from the landing place. The duties of these patrols will be to keep in close touch with the enemy to ascertain and report his movements, and prevent his reconnoitring parties from getting through'.

Bicycles continued in service in the British army and were used during World War II in a number of theatres. There were two sorts of machine referred to as 'Trade' cycles and 'Folding' cycles. The former were machines supplied by the trade to their normal civilian specifications but painted khaki and the latter were specially designed folding bicycles made to military specifications. Cycles of these sorts were used by the airborne troops and a divisional allocation was 1,907

'Trade' and 1,362 folding machines. In the Irish army between the two world wars, there was even an entire cavalry regiment mounted on bicycles.

In France, the army had bicycles during the 1880's these being ordinaries but in 1896 they adopted the folding bicycle designed by a certain Captain Gérard. This machine had the saddle mounted over the back wheel with the pedals just in front of the rear wheel with a short chain. The frame was two bars which folded in the centre. The machine was designed to be carried on the back of the soldier and was fitted with two straps, similar to knapsack straps which passed over the shoulder. The French continued with this pattern until 1940.

Little use was made of the bicycle during the Russo-Japanese War by either side but it was used by Greek, Bulgarian and Serbian troops during the Balkan Wars in 1912 and 1913, but the general course of operations did not lend itself to any great use of the machine. The Italians, made use of their type of military cycle during their campaign in Tripoli with, it seems, some measure of success.

Germany, as can be expected was quick off the mark with a specially designed military machine. The pattern they adopted at the end of the nineteenth century was a folding type similar in appearance to the French pattern with the saddle mounted directly over the rear wheel. It differed from the French pattern in having the two central bars of the frame farther apart and strengthened with a central plate and two uprights just in front of the folding point. The German army during World War II had cyclist battalions and these were used after the invasion on D-Day to speedily move troops to strengthen defences against the Allied advance. The Japanese used the bicycle with spectacular success during the invasion on Malaya and the capture of Singapore when they rode through what was considered impenetrable jungle each soldier armed with not only his rifle and equipment and bag of rice but holding firecrackers to create the impression that their force was greater in size than it actually was. It worked and the British forces withdrew and Malaya and Singapore fell to the enemy.

Recent military use of the bicycle was against the French in Indo-China when the Viet Minh pressed bicycles into service to ferry supplies of food and ammunition to the front line troops around Dien Bien Phu. By the time the battle started, thousands of men and their machines had stockpiled rice, other foods and ammunition ready for the assault. The French were unable, even with their air force to bomb the transport with any success as the narrow cycle tracks through the jungle were invisible from the air and offered no target as a road would do. Perhaps the most ironic part of the whole war, was that the bicycles on which the Viet Minh depended so much were made in France by Peugeot.

In the recent Vietnam war, the bicycle was again used by the Communist forces to ferry supplies and ammunition to the troops and because of the nature of the country, as the French found, so did the Americans that it was almost impossible to pinpoint cycle paths in the jungle from the air. However, an American journalist who returned from Vietnam in 1967 stated that he believed that without their bicycles, the enemy would have to abandon the war.

But it was not just guerrillas who used the machine for supplies and movement. The military bicycle was used in Crete in 1958 by men of the Royal Horse Guards on patrol against the E.O.K.A. forces on the island.

6

The Bicycle Since 1900

The safety machine which was prevalent at the beginning of the reign of Edward VII was a simple machine by previous standards but still it was adapted for the various uses it was called upon to perform. While manufacturers turned out their standard models, they also produced *de luxe* items, made-to-measure and to order. There were still a smattering of other makers assembling their designs from standard parts of other manufacturers incorporating improvements and pet innovations of their own. However, although the motor car had arrived on the scene, another invention derived from the internal combustion engine had already made its appearance. As early as 1869 the famous Pierre Michaux had fitted a Perreau steam-engine to one of his boneshakers to improve the machine and give effortless but probably not trouble-free riding. (He did leave the pedals in case of emergency.) This machine, because of the development we have already followed obviously had little impact on the cycling market but in 1885, Gottlieb Daimler fitted an ingenious internal combustion engine to a bicycle with two small balancing wheels, as may be found today on children's machines, which lifted once the motorized cycle moved off. It was not, however, until the safety bicycle was popular that a serious and practical attempt was made to fit engines. From these beginnings was born the motorcycle which is another fascinating subject that cannot be discussed here (see *Motorcycles in Colour* by Eric Thompson. Blandford Press).

To return to the safety bicycle which had by now pervaded all levels of society and was proving a cheap and effective transport for countless numbers of people. With the improvements in roads in Britain, Europe and America, the safety was seen in vast quantities. While the safety was a commendable two-wheeled machine its versatility was astounding. It could be adapted for postal deliveries, and by means of wicker chairs over the top part of the front wheel stretching from the handlebars be used to carry children. With a large wicker basket on the front it was an ideal machine for shopping but above all it was a means of leisure, hitherto unimagined.

The safety machines used in Europe, in Germany, France, Holland and Scandinavia were, although made by national manufacturers, derived from and followed the designs of the British makers. But while the bicycle was a social pastime it was for many an essential social necessity. It speeded up rural life, it helped doctors, policemen, postmen and others and it gave the working man a cheap form of conveyance to and from his place of employment enabling him to live farther from it. While these were important economic factors, one main social advantage was that it allowed people in the overcrowded cities, especially the industrial cities and towns to escape into the country on Sundays and the roads during the Edwardian period up to World War I were crowded with people pursuing a peaceful pastime and breathing fresh air.

The safety of the first decade of the twentieth century demonstrated, thanks to the designs and efforts of many creative people various important refinements and accessories.

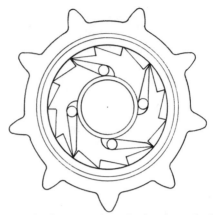

The free wheel, standard item on bicycles by the end of the nineteenth century.

The improvements came thick and fast in the years leading up to World War I and affected every part of the machine and improved either safety or efficiency. By the turn of the century, free wheel was firmly established and the back pedalling rim brake as we have seen in Chapter IV; pneumatic tyres were the *only* tyres worth having and gears had made their appearance.

The most important advance made was the introduction of the gears on cycles. Rudimentary gears had been designed in the 1890's and in Plate 88, the gearing of this special pacing machine for racing cyclists was provided by a 20 in. cogged wheel. The most significant and important, and still retained system of gearing was the Sturmey-Archer three-speed hub patented in 1902 by Henry Sturmey and James Archer. The manufacture of this gearing system was undertaken by Raleigh. Because of its cheapness of manufacture and its relative simplicity it was soon one of the favoured gearing systems. Others were not, however, to be put off, and produced their own designs. There was the three-speed Armstrong-Triplex patented in 1906 by A. Reilly, the three-speed gear patented in 1902 by M. Pedersen for use on the

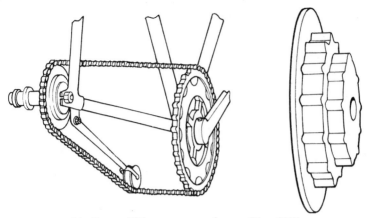

Lindley and Biggs two-speed gear. *Circa* 1900.

Dursley-Pedersen machine. Another gear was invented by A. Eadie in 1903 but all these were of the enclosed hub or epicyclic type, and many, although excellent in design and performance soon disappeared in favour of the Sturmey-Archer hub. This was improved with the introduction of a four-speed type in 1938 and today (1978) a five-speed type is available.

The epicyclic hub consisted of a set of gears contained inside the large rear hub of the machine and the drive transmitted from the pedals to the rear sprocket of the hub could be altered by selecting one of the gears required. Selection was by various means such as a small lever on the handlebars or mounted on the crossbar or even by twisting the grip. These controls were connected to the change gear mechanism by cable.

The other form of gear was the derailleur gear system, the first modern and practical form of which appeared in France in 1909. The derailleur, from the French meaning derail, worked exactly on that principle. The free wheel hub was fitted with from two to six interchangeable cogged sprocket wheels of differing diameters to give the required gearing and a device which allowed the chain to be 'derailed' from one to another. Because of the differences in the size of the various gear sprockets a sprung device was provided to take up the slack of the chain. The forerunner of this type of gear was the system invented by Lindley and Biggs in about 1900. This two-speed gear had a specially shaped chain which passed over a wide wheel fitted with pedals at the front and a specially designed rear wheel with two sizes of cogged wheels as part of it. This special chain allowed the gear to change from the larger to the smaller or vice versa rear hub thus altering the gearing ratio. In order to maintain constant tension on the driving chain a sprung lever with pulley was fitted which by its action took up the slack when on the lower gear.

Other improvements to the bicycle at this period and during the late 1890's were however more frivolous than effective. One such patent referred to 'a device for protecting the hands of the cyclist against cold' dating from 1897. This, taken out by the author's great grandmother referred to a pair of gauntlets 'more particularly adapted to ladies' use' attached to the handlebar of the machine. To activate bell and brake, suitable openings were provided, protected with glove-like fingers in leather. Other types of hand protectors were also patented and manufactured and as well as these, the

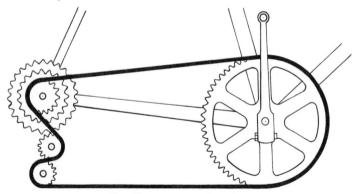

Derailleur system of gearing.

more serious-minded cyclist started to fit his or her machine with a number of necessary accessories. The most significant was the brake, and these included rim brakes of various types, the clipper rim brake, and the stirrup rim and the contracting brake activated by levers and rods or the now important Bowden Cable or the hub type brakes worked by furious back pedalling on the part of the cyclist. All these replaced the earlier forms of brakes which had survived, if they were fitted from the days of the boneshaker and the ordinary. These brakes on the former machine were wood blocks which pressed hard on the rear wheel while the ordinary brakes, while employing this method modified it slightly and employed a shaped roller as the rear brake. This in turn gave rise to the so-called 'spoon' brake which pressed on the front tyre being activated by pressure on the lever fitted to the handlebar. This far from effective system, especially if a puncture occurred gave way to the new designs mentioned above. It was not, however, for some years that brakes were fitted to both front and rear wheels.

Another most essential accessory with the pneumatic tyre was a puncture outfit and a pump of some kind. These came in various shapes and sizes (see Plate 103) until the pump we know today became the standard type.

For the serious cyclist there was the essential cyclometer or mileometer which told the cyclist the number of miles he had covered. These fitted to the hub and recorded the mileage on a small clock-like face. One such ingenious machine actually provided the nocturnal cyclist with a special improvement that 'pinged' every mile to allow the cyclist in the dark to calculate the length of his journey.

There was also the lamp fitted to the cycle for night riding. These had been fitted to ordinaries, hanging precariously from the front hub between the cage of spokes and usually powered by a candle, or oil. In 1896, the firm of Joseph Lucas produced perhaps their most famous cycle lamp named 'King of the Road'. This lamp consisted of an oil reservoir, a glass-covered reflector and a wick holder. The sides of the lamp were provided with coloured lenses, red for port and green for starboard! In 1898, this form of lamp was overtaken (although they were still advertised by Lucas as late as 1940) by the new acetylene lamp. This new form of lamp had a carbide reservoir at the base and a water one at the top. The action of the water on the carbide formed a gas that burned with a bright flame. Later the first dynamo adapted for cycles was produced by the Swiss. This worked on the rotating back wheel to supply power to the electric front and rear lights. These replaced the battery and acetylene lamps in many cases, but the latter still continued in use for many years. Plate 103 shows a selection of cycle lamps, cyclometers and in the foreground an ingenious foot pump for tyres.

The last essential 'extra' the cyclist needed for his machine was the warning system. They previously used horns, bugles, whistles and suchlike and had by the turn of the century been superseded by the simple bell which still survives to this day. Fitted conveniently on the handlebar of the cycle within easy reach of the thumb to work the mechanism, it became the universal cyclist warning system.

From 1900 until the end of the first quarter of the new century the bicycle did not change at all in design and was produced by a slowly decreasing number of companies. The decline in the use of the bicycle can be attributed directly to the motor car and the motorcycle which by the early 1920's were fairly cheap to buy.

The cycle boom with the coming of the safety had affected other countries besides Britain. In France there was an upsurge in the use of cycles as there was in Belgium, Germany, Holland and Scandinavia. In Germany the industrialized cities of the Ruhr saw the bicycle as the most convenient form of transport for the vast work forces operating in concerns such as Krupps and Farben and throughout Europe and Britain the cycle was the most convenient form of transport for the working man. Factories in various cities and towns constructed cycle sheds and parks for their work forces and some countries provided special cycle ways for the cyclist.

In America, the boom that had gripped other countries was also felt. As in Britain and Germany as well as Belgium and France arms manufacturers in America entered the market, the most notable being Remington who like others in Britain also entered the typewriter market. In America, the discerning customer could choose from the Remington cycle, the Rambler, the Crescent, and the Sterling which boasted in its advertisements that the Sterling front fork was 'built like a watch'! Victor cycles were also in evidence as well as the Tribune cycle, which the company proudly proclaimed as 'the most popular high grade Bicycle in the world' adding that at the time the fastest mile had been accomplished by C. M. Murphy on it, who, riding behind a train with a suitable wind guard, had achieved a mile in 57.8 seconds. The advertising of cycles followed the same pattern in both America and Europe, each manufacturer pointing out the astounding feats of his machine, its versatility, its strength and ease of ride, its cheapness and its *de luxe* finish – but the Chicago Ice Bicycle Apparatus Company boasted a most novel machine. Destined presumably for the icy wastes of Alaska this safety machine had a suitably chained rear wheel for drive and a front 'ski' fitted where the front wheel should be. Undoubtedly this proved a formidable machine in icy conditions.

There was, however, very little change in the design of the bicycle in spite of efforts of a few. In 1895, the Bamboo Cycle Company launched their safety which was a conventional machine which replaced straight tube framing, but not the joints with poles of male bamboo (female bamboo is partially hollow and so unsuitable while male bamboo is solid and used, for example, for lances) announcing that it was 'better than steel' and added as a gentle reminder to the would-be purchaser that it was 'patronized by the nobility'. Other additional items soon became available for the safety cyclist. He could, if desired, fit a side-car to his machine to take a wife or passenger and if a family owned a tandem then the same side-car could be fitted for the offpsring of the family. On the other hand, for the lucky man to own a safety machine, for courting, or in the other extreme, for taking mother shopping, and who could not afford this luxury, there was always the wicker trailer which could be hired for 1s. (5p) per week (Plate 91). This addition to the safety (whichever pattern) meant that the machine was capable of carrying two people without the expense of two machines, a tandem or a side-car. Most safetys at this period fitted a tubular socket just below the saddle to take the trail of this additional item.

The safety also permitted more efficient commercial delivery machines, such as those shown in Plates 93 and 94 which were typical of their type and the G.P.O. also had their parcel delivery cycles with red painted wicker baskets on the front. Although essentially tricycles, the machines employed the back half as it were of the safety cycle.

The tricycle still survived, however, in spite of the popularity of the safety cycle and surprisingly the sociable cycling also continued up to World War I. Various machines were manufactured including the sociable of 1914 with a single front wheel steered by the gentleman and a false set of handlebars for the lady. It is interesting to note from the machine shown in Plate 80 that the rear portions are a gents' and ladies' safety machine. Others went even further and possibly to absurd lengths, the prime example being the sociable which employed a gents' and ladies' safety cycle and joined them with crossbars to make a sociable. The handlebars were linked for steering but this depended very much on whether the two riders agreed about direction. The other problem was that the propulsion was also independent.

The tricycle in the years before and after World War I provided sedate travel for ladies shopping (Plate 86) and a suitable machine for young children. Although its popularity was on the decline, racing machines of this type continued to be popular during the 1930's when tandem racing and racing with additional numbers were also at their zenith.

As in other forms of sport to do with transportation the machine purchased from shops was improved by the attention paid by manufacturers to the machine they put on the track or in a race. The earlier forms of racing already mentioned were a twofold venture, primarily to publicize a machine rather than test and improve on it, although early makers for their own sakes kept a firm eye on the mechanical performance of their machines. The most famous of cycle races started in 1903 was the Tour de France, an around France cycle race in stages. Sponsored by two Parisian newspapers, the race offered a suitable testing ground for the cycle trade and for the first years of the race, competition was between manufacturers. Later in 1930 this was changed to a national competition. In Britain cycle races were also organized, the most famous being the Tour of Britain started in 1951 and sponsored as in the Tour de France by a national newspaper. In 1955 the race sponsorship was taken over by the Milk Marketing Board and inevitably the race was dubbed 'The Milk Race'.

The Tour de France had been a predominantly French and Italian race, perhaps more French than the latter but in 1953 a British team was entered which completed the course. In 1977, Raleigh scored a resounding victory for the British cycle industry by winning the overall team prize and having, after a gruelling battle, the second place rider.

Besides road racing there was still the popular sport of track and the newer stadium racing, each of which produced their champions with fast times and allowed the manufacturers to evolve lightweight design machines for the race track which eventually influenced the design of the cycle bought in the shop.

The breakthrough of improvments to the weight of cycles came in the 1920's when the Rudge-Whitworth concern produced its light roadster machine which employed high tensile yet light tubes for the frame. A great improvement was made in soldering and brazing of the component tubes and the parts that required the weight of both ladies' and gents' machines. This improvement in construction techniques also affected the tandem which during the late 1930's found a family and popular market for cheap and efficient touring and holiday use.

While most manufacturers, happy with their new mode of lightweight manufacture continued to produce the machines whose design had been stabilized in the early decades of the twentieth century, there were those who looked in other directions for the continued development of the bicycle. In Italy in the 1930's a manufacturer produced the 'Velocino' which although the manufacturer claimed that it was an advancement appears to have been a retrograde step in cycle development. While the design was particularly nineteenth century in appearance, the Velocino did have a number of revolutionary points about its design. It had a large rear wheel and a small front one for steering, reminiscent of the old sociables; had the saddle mounted over the rear wheel and the cogged drive wheel over the front wheel connecting with the rear wheel by a chain and gears. The steering was perhaps the most old-fashioned system of the new machine. This involved two separate arms, each encompassing the rider and connected to a central steering column. While it was claimed to be easily stored, the inventors claim of ease of dismounting in an emergency could, from the design, lead to a nasty accident.

World War II, was, for the civilian, the bicycle war, when petrol was rationed and when speed and silence of movement was necessary. As in World War I, bicycles were provided for the military and used by troops, resistance fighters and airborne troops, although the prevalence of the motorcycle produced for the armed forces a more efficient if noisier machine.

98

The post-war years, while again because of rationing of petrol allowing a growth of the cycle market, did again not produce anything different in design. Bicycles have a sturdy and long life and many a machine sold in the 1920's and even before, were used in the late 1940's and 1950's and many of these machines are still in use today. Requiring the minimum of maintenance, cycles if over forty or so years old still perform and are still perfectly functional.

While the so-called 'classic' style of machine influenced perhaps by racing with dropped handlebars are still the mainstay of cycle makers, a new style of machine, perhaps more adapted to modern urban life appeared in 1962. While the design was revolutionary and it has been improved on since, along the same principles, it was first in theory thought of during the 1940's. Sir Alliot Vernon-Roe, perhaps better known for his pioneering work in aviation designed a machine using modern lightweight metals, yet with the old crossframe design which had been ousted by the diamond frame of Humber and universally used by cycle manufacturers.

Bicycle manufacture had during the years preceding the war and the years after, fallen into a conservative rut. The many manufacturers both pre- and post-war (those who had survived) were swallowed up by Raleigh. Such names as Humber, Rudge-Whitworth, Triumph, B.S.A. and others found themselves part of the vast empire for it was the only way that the industry could survive.

While the established designs continued to roll off the production line and find, in spite of the car and motorcycle, a ready market, designers still tried to improve on the basic 'safety'. As we have seen, the Italian Velocino was a poor answer and in the war years, an American company, while patriotic in thought, produced an even poorer answer. The machine designed by an American piano-making company used laminated wood for the frame, forks and every component except for pedals, cogs, and driving chains. The design never caught on and vanished into oblivion, joining perhaps the previously mentioned 'Bamboo' bicycle!

Vernon-Roe while not successful with its design of cross-framed machines did however spark off a revolution in cycle design that cannot and was not ignored. The crossframe design, however, needed to be explored further and the man that did this was Alex Moulton in 1962.

Moulton's design had first developed in 1959 in prototype form and with its new concept in design, style and size could have revolutionized the market at a time when the cycle industry was in the doldrums. The new machine had small wheels, the tubes of the frame were flat sided and the small wheels were compensated by a novel suspension system. Moulton, at first offered his design to Raleigh who rejected it as a commercial venture, and not to be deterred, Moulton formed his own company to manufacture his machine.

In 1962, it appeared and soon the production capacity set up was proved to be inadequate. Such was the runaway success of the cycle that Moulton undertook production at an under-capacity B.M.C. plant and produced his machine and in addition a folding model. In 1967, Raleigh, having seen the enormous success of the machine they had been offered, purchased the patent rights and manufactured and improved on the original machine. Examples of this style are now made for children and adults alike and the latest development along this line of folding machine is the Bickerton bicycle, yet another advance in cycle design.

While some might consider that the bicycle has reached its full and effective evolution in design and performance, the same was said 100 years ago when Starley produced the 'Ariel', and perhaps even earlier when 'Hobby horse' gave way to 'Boneshaker' and that in turn gave way to the 'Ordinary'. The 'Safety' was proclaimed as the ultimate and perhaps for decades it was, but man's inventive nature can and will surely produce in the years to come yet further improvements to the cycle.

1 Hobby horse. 1818.

2 Hobby horse. 1818.

3 Child's hobby
horse. 1819.

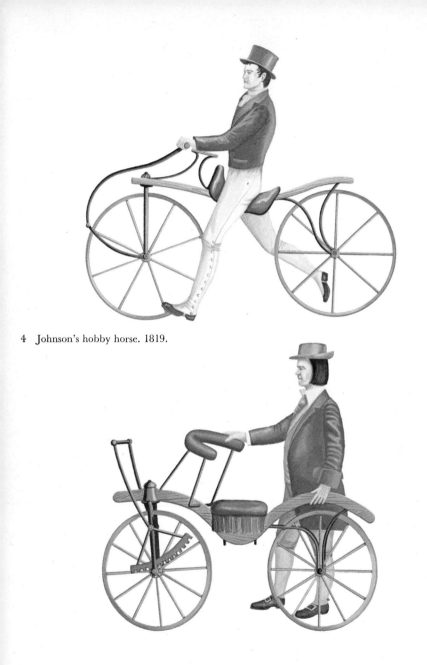

4 Johnson's hobby horse. 1819.

5 Gompertz's velocipede. 182

Von Drais's Draisenne. 1818.

Lady's Accelerator or Pilentum. 1819.

8 Copy of the Macmillan velocipede. c. 186(

9 Drais improved velocipede. 18

Macmillan type machine. 1860.

Willard Sawyer velocipede quadricycle. 1851.

12 Quadricycle made for Prince Albert. 18

13 Singer tricycle. 18

Boneshaker bicycle. 1869.

Samuel Webb Thomas's lady's machine. 1870.

16 French boneshaker. 18

Boneshaker tricycle. 1869.

Boneshaker tricycle. 1869.

19 Boneshaker bicycle. 1868.

20 Boneshaker tandem tricycle. 186

1 Boy's boneshaker bicycle. 1869.

2 Lady's and child's boneshaker bicycles. 1869.

23   Needham tricycle. 18

Pickering's velocipede. 1868.

25 Boneshaker bicycle. 1

Ariel men's and lady's bicycles. 1872.

27 Ordinary bicycle.

28 Ordinary bicycle.

Ordinary bicycle. 1882.

Detail of rear brake. 1882.

31 Ordinary bicycle. 18█

32 Singer Xtraordinary bicycle. 1878.

33 Rudge rotary tricycle. 1878.

34 Quadrant tricycle. 1880.

35 American velocipede. 186

Lawson safety bicycle. 1876.

Shergold safety bicycle. 1876.

'Kangaroo' dwarf ordinary bicycle. 1885.

40 Hemming's unicycle. 18

1 Rudge quad triplet. 1881.

Bayliss and Thomas tandem tricycle. 1882.

43 Warwick monarch caddy. 188

44 Detail of rear suspensio

Bayliss and Thomas folding tricycle. 1881.

46   Bayliss and Thomas folding tricycle. 1881.

47 Tricycle with double cogged rear. 18

48 Starley tricycle. 18

Carrouch tricycle. 1880.

Cheylesmore tricycle. 1880.

51 Coventry machinists' tricycle. 1878.

52 Rudge sociable tricycle. 1878.

53 Norfolk tricycle. 1888.

54   Singer poster. 1880s.

55   Howe poster.

56 Tandem tricycle. 18

Rover safety bicycle. 1884.

B.S.A. safety bicycle. 1884.

59　Humber safety bicycle. 18

60　Second Rover safety bicycle. 18

Premier safety bicycle. 1885.

Raleigh safety bicycle. 1888.

Evening Standard

THURSDAY MARCH 9TH

IMPERIAL PARLIAME
Mr GLADSTONES SPEECH
LORD RANDOLPH CHURCHILL
SOCIALIST OF BOW

JO PENN ACCUSED
OF MAKING A DRAWING

UNIVERSITY BOAT RACE

TRAM STRIKE IN NEW YORK

CHOP HOUSE DOOMED

JULES VERNE SHOT

THE CARRIER

Rudge quadricycle. 1888.

Olympia tandem tricycle. 1890.

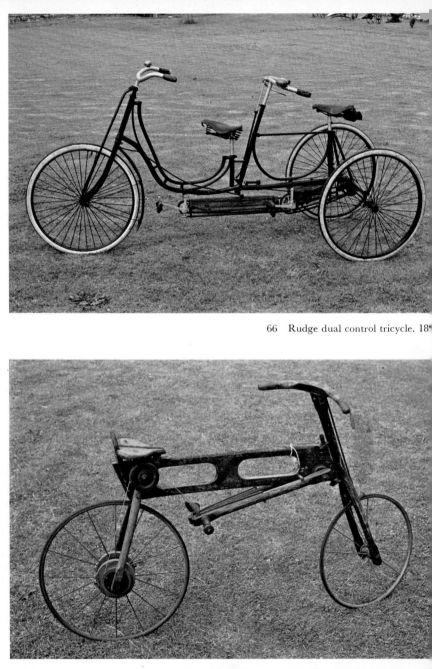

66 Rudge dual control tricycle. 18?

67 German Mergamobile. 18?

Tricycle. 1900.

Child's horse tricycle. 1890s.

70   Child's tricycle. 189

71   Child's tricycle. 19

Lawson's 'bicyclette'. 1879.

Bamboo bicycle. 1895.

74   Safety bicycle. 189

75   Elswick lady's safety bicycle. 189

Military bicycle. 1896.

77   Dursley Pedersen bicycle. 190[

78   Safety bicycle. 190[

Kendrick tricycle. 1914.

Sociable tricycle. 1914.

81 Crypto Bantam. 18

82 Rover shaft-drive bicycle. 19

Rover shaft-drive lady's bicycle. 1910.

Detail of shaft drive.

85 Ariel quint. 18

86 Ladies' tricycle. 19

Chater Lea tandem. 1910.

Chater Lea pacing machine. 1898.

89　Ladies' safety. 19

90　Triumph safety with side-car. 19

Raleigh Carefree with wicker trailer. 1912.

Referee safety bicycle. 1901.

93 Milk delivery tricycle. 19

94 Delivery tricycle. 19

5   Golden Sunbeam safety bicycle. 1915.

6   Tricycle. 1910.

97 Folding BSA bicycle. 1915

98 Folding BSA bicycle, folded. 1915

Folding BSA military bicycle. 1940.

Kendrick racing tricycle. 1930s.

101 Indian soldier with military bicycle. 19

2 Types of saddles.

3 Cycle lamps. Cyclometers. Tyre pump.

104 Plaques of cycle manufacturers.

105 Peugeot Sports special. 1977.

9   Raleigh Scrambler Trike. 1977.

110   Raleigh Nova bicycle. 197

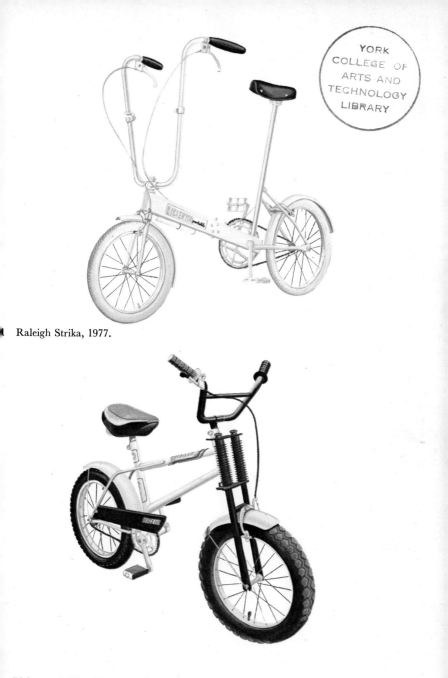

Raleigh Strika, 1977.

Bickerton folding bicycle. 1977.

113 Raleigh Stowaway. 19

Plate Descriptions

Plate 1 – Hobby Horse. 1818. This plate shows the general style of the hobby horse at this early period. The wood wheels are shod with iron tyres and the forks holding both front and rear wheel are adjustable to allow for differing lengths of leg. This was done by the simple method of having a number of corresponding holes in the front and rear forks and moving the wheel up and down between the fork to attain the desired height. The frame is a simple wood bar with leather-covered padded saddle in front of which is the chest rest to enable the rider to lean forward and so exert more pressure on the road with his feet and gain more speed. The steering on this model is direct by a simple crossbar and grip with central rod to the front fork.

Plate 2 – Hobby Horse, 1818. This plate shows another version of the popular hobby horse. This version does not have adjustable wheels and was therefore specially made to suit a certain person. The frame is less well designed than that shown in Plate 1 and the wheels of the same rather than differing sizes. The block to the front of the rather inadequate saddle should hold the chest rest which is now missing. Steering differed from the machine shown in Plate 1 and was by the long rod arrangement which can be seen curving down to the hub of the front wheel. After 1820 adjustment for height on this form of machine was by raising or lowering the saddle rather than adjusting the length of fork.

Plate 3 – Child's hobby horse. 1819. This elaborately

carved machine was obviously specially commissioned by someone of means to be used by their son in and around the grounds of a large house. The carved frame forms the saddle portion and is without chest rest as speed was presumably not of importance. Steering is direct and the rear and front wheels held between iron forks of some considerable size and weight. It is doubtful if a child could have covered any distance on this machine and it was intended purely as a plaything.

Plate 4 – Johnson's hobby horse. 1819. Taken from a contemporary print of the celebrated first rider on the hobby horse, it shows the riding 'dress' of the more conservative and differs from those shown in Plates 1 and 2 in having larger size wheels, a more comfortable saddle and a shaped frame of wood. The chest rest can also clearly be seen in front of the rider. Steering is indirect similar to the style shown in Plate 2 and from contemporary illustrations seems to have been the most popular form. Johnson who patented his design of machine in 1818 not only manufactured them for resale but set up a riding school in Soho to teach the art of hobby horse riding. Being a keen businessman, Johnson also hired machines for those not rich enough to own one.

Plate 5 – Gompertz's velocipede. 1821. The first real breakthrough in the history of the cycle was made by Louis Gompertz who increased efficiency and speed by combining both leg and arm power. The machine while basically conforming to the general layout of the hobby horse with wood frame – this time a little more shaped, iron forks for the equal-sized front and rear wheels and padded saddle – had a novel form of front-wheel drive. It will be noticed from the illustration that the saddle chest rest is much higher than previously and this was to aid the driver in using his arms to propel and steer the front wheel which could have been no mean feat. Once the machine was underway in the hobby horse style, the arms pushed back and forth on the crossbar which moved the ratcheted arc over the cogged hub and gave extra propulsion to the machine. However, unluckily for Gompertz his idea never caught on and until the 1860's more of the inventors' energy was concentrated on machines with four wheels.

Plate 6 – Von Drais's Draisenne. 1818. This machine, the brainchild of Baron von Drais appeared in Paris in 1818 and predated the hobby horses we have already seen. Developed from the early *célérifères*, von Drais dispensed with the carved animal heads and even bodies, substituted a basic wood frame and wheel and fitted the front wheel in such a way that it pivoted. This was done with a single coach bolt, washer and nut. While he attracted much publicity, which he seems to have revelled in,. von Drais was taken seriously by some and sold quite a number of his machines. It was from the von Drais machine that Johnson developed his much-improved machine in England.

Plate 7 – Lady's Accelerator or Pilentum. 1819. Ladies were, of course, not considered with this new form of transport and so some channelled their ideas into producing a suitable, elegant and accepted mode of self-propulsion. This machine, variations of which appeared in the early 1820's, was deemed the answer. It was, however, more of a plaything than a serious mode of transport. The machine illustrated was powered by the treadle action shown. These combined with a hand action revolved the cranks fitted to the front wheel. Contemporary prints, one of which was the inspiration for this plate, show the machine against a country house and grounds setting and it was here rather than the open road that this form of machine was used for a few short turns around the estate. While some contemporary prints, mainly of a satirical nature show women riding hobby horses, one famous one being entitled 'The Female Race', it is highly unlikely that women usually used such machines.

Plate 8 – Copy of Macmillan velocipede. c. 1860. Although this machine dates from around 1860, it was according to the now long-deceased maker, a replica of the original machine developed by Macmillan in the early 1840's. Made by Thomas McCall, a joiner and wheelwright, from what he claimed were original plans, the machine has a larger rear than front wheel, a low dropped type of frame, and sprung saddle with rear protecting guard just behind it. The handlebars turned the front wheel, but to a limited angle each side so the machine had a poor turning circle. The lack of turning power was due to the method of propulsion. The rear wheel was fitted with cranks which were operated by rod and treadles at the front and it was the arms of the treadles fitted to the front forks of the frame that hampered the turning powers of the machine. This can be clearly understood from the illustration. Despite the advances made in the design of the hobby horse, Macmillan, or perhaps it was McCall could not refrain from having a carved horse's head on the front of the machine. McCall set himself up to manufacture these machines and made a few retailing at £7 each. Others (see Plate 10) also adopted the treadle theory but adapted to all-metal machines.

Plate 9 – Drais improved velocipede. 1832. This was an attempt, if perhaps at the wrong time when the interest in this form of machine was declining, to revive the cycle. The improved machine was hardly an improvement and by its very appearance was cumbersome and difficult to ride and steer. The steering was complicated and while the improvements included adjustable saddle and arm or chest rest, mechanically it had very little to offer and died a natural death.

Plate 10 – Macmillan type machine. c. 1860. This machine while from a mechanical point of view similar to the Macmillan and McCall machine the rear wheel is larger than the front wheel and the steering is direct but perhaps the most significant improvement was the adjustable treadle rods which allowed the foot rests to be moved to differing positions. The machine illustrated is incomplete and lacks the supporting arms from the rear of the saddle to perhaps the back hub, or even the frame which acted as a rudimentary form of comfort and suspension. This is a prime example of the many locally made machines by blacksmiths and wheelwrights to designs either seen in journals or even concocted by those who ordered them to be made.

Plate 11 – Willard Sawyer velocipedes quadricycle. 1851. This machine is one of the rarest of its type and perhaps the most preserved and unique example of the work of Willard Sawyer. Made in 1851 at Dover where the works were situated, the machine has hickory spokes to the wheels, and a treadle action to propel the rear wheels by a system of cranks. Steering was by a single central front arm. A number of these machines were made by Sawyer, who incorporated sophisticated means of manufacture into his products. The wrought iron crankshaft which can be seen at the front of the machine with its four bearings was a masterpiece of ironwork. Sawyer retailed these machines for £17 2s. 6d. (£17.12½p approx.) and exhibited one of the machines at the Great Exhibition in 1851.

Plate 12 – Quadricycle made for Prince Albert. 1851. While outwardly similar to the previous machine described made by Sawyer in the same year, this specially commissioned quadricycle made by J. Ward of Leicester Square in London for Prince Albert has one or two differing features. The rear wheels on this machine are larger than those at the front and the treadle system slightly more cumbersome. Also by comparison the wheels are stronger and heavier in design with less spokes but perhaps the main difference is the quality of workmanship. The Sawyer machine is a perfect example of this maker's attention to detail and quality while the Ward machine although technically well made shows little of the craftsmanship of the other machine. Sawyer was perhaps slightly disappointed having exhibited at the Great Exhibition in 1851 instigated by the Prince to see such a machine ordered from another manufacturer.

Plate 13 – Singer tricycle. 1879. Although slightly out of context, this Singer machine of the late 1870's shows little mechanical improvement on early crank-driven models. While the wheels, frame and general layout had been evolved, the cumbersome and often tiresome crank drive by treadles had been retained. Coming as it did at the beginning of the 'Ordinary' or 'Penny-Farthing' era, the influence on design are obvious at a glance. Steering was accomplished by the use of the two wooden-handled levers on the front and the top of the front forks were fitted with suitable clips on which lamps could be placed.

Plate 14 – Boneshaker bicycle. 1869. This boneshaker or velocipede was built in England by W. Hedges in 1869. It was typical of many machines of this type made both by cycle manufacturers and by local wheelwrights, blacksmiths and coachbuilders. The front wheel was larger than the back and made from wood in the traditional way with an iron frame and forks to both wheels and a saddle on a lighter back connected to the rear hub that gave a small if somewhat inadequate form of suspension. The shoe-type brake was fitted to the rear wheel and like coach brakes was a block of wood mounted on an iron bed and pivoted at the centre. This was connected to the handlebars by a piece of thin rope or cord and the handlebars made to twist. When the handlebars were gripped by the rider and twisted towards him, this motion shortened the cord and pulled the wooden brake block on to the iron tyre of the rear wheel. Propulsion was direct by means of pedals fitted to the hub of the front wheel.

Plate 15 – Samuel Webb Thomas's lady's machine. 1870. This formidable and somewhat weighty machine was manufactured in 1870. It was an early attempt to allow women to ride bicycles without losing any respect and so it was made side-saddle. The frame was 'S' shaped to allow the front wheel to be positioned over on to the right side and the rear wheel with saddle over to the left. The saddle was that fitted to the more sedate quadricycles and the wheels were protected with wicker or network to avoid the unseemly entanglement of a lady's dress. The propulsion was by means of double crank pedals fitted to the front wheel.

Plate 16 – French boneshaker. 1868. Although this is a man's machine, the daring French lady in her 'rational' dress revealing for the time a scandalous amount of leg seems to be quite at ease on probably what is a Michaux machine. The illustration taken from a contemporary photograph shows the rear wheel brake and the sprung saddle. While totally unacceptable in English Victorian society, the *risqué* costume was possibly just about accepted in Paris. While most boneshakers conformed to roughly the same design, there were always variations because of the different manufacturers.

Plate 17 – Boneshaker tricycle. 1869. This machine was made by T. Clarke and shows clearly how the boneshaker bicycle was adapted and made into a tricycle. The same front wheel and handlebar arrangement was retained but the frame was differently shaped. It sloped down from the front and divided into two to support the rear axle and wheels. The saddle was situated on a separate piece of iron which split into two forks at the rear and connected with the rear wheels and axle. This type of machine was popular amongst the elder and more conservative followers of the sport as it was considered safer and more sedate to ride one.

Plate 18 – Boneshaker tricycle. 1869. This is an example of a locally made boneshaker manufactured by a Mr West of Benson, Oxfordshire, the local wheelwright and blacksmith. It differs slightly from the previous illustration in having the frame dividing into three at the rear, larger front and rear wheels and no front wheel brake. Boneshakers were also manufactured and used in America and France and in America, one of the leading companies who sold boneshaker tricycles was Bramhall Smith and Co. of New York.

Plate 19 – Boneshaker bicycle. 1868. This is yet another example of the boneshaker, again differing slightly in some of the minor points. This machine, for example, has adjustable pedals that can be moved up and down the bar to suit the length of the legs of the rider. This example is also equipped with foot-rests which can be seen at the very end of the frame in front of the handlebars. When travelling at speed, which was usually downhill, the rider raised his feet from the fast revolving pedals and placed them on the foot-rests. When normal speed was resumed which one hopes was possible with the rather ineffectual brake, the feet were returned to the pedals.

Plate 20 – Boneshaker tandem tricycle. 1869. This rare and most unusual machine was made by J. Child of Barnet. This most ingenious machine is not unusual in being a two-seater and a tricycle, but both riders were expected to contribute to the propulsion. The front rider who sat in the saddle in the normal way pedalled on conventional boneshaker pedals on the front wheel but the rear passenger who was lower down and rather slung behind turned the cranked rear axle by hand! Naturally perfect co-ordination between riders was essential if the work load was to be equally shared. The front wheel was equipped with the usual wood block brake activated by twisting the handlebars. The machine also has an elaborate coach lamp mounted on the side.

Plate 21 – Boy's boneshaker bicycle. 1869. This unusual machine was one of a set made in Lewes by the local wheelwright and blacksmith to the order of the Rev. G. Bates. The entire collection and as the following plate shows as well consisted of a ladies' model, a gents' model, a boys' model and a child's version. The boy's version has the usual arrangement of the boneshaker but an unusually small rear wheel. A brake, now missing, operated on the front wheel by twisting the handlebars.

Plate 22 – Ladies' and child's boneshaker bicycles. c. 1869. Both these machines were made to the order of the Rev. G. Bates of Lewes for his family. The ladies' model, similar to the machine shown in Plate 15 is a side-saddle version with 'S' shaped frame and wicker to protect the dress from becoming entangled with the spokes of the wheel. As can be seen from the plates, these machines were painted various colours and it appears that the Rev. Bates preferred his family machines to be blue with white coach lines as shown in the lady's machine, recently restored. The child's machine, a most unusual and rare machine of its type follows the same design as that shown in Plate 21 but on this machine there was no brake. From the weight of the child's boneshaker it is difficult to imagine the small rider covering much distance on it.

Plate 23 – Needham tricycle. 1869. This boneshaker tandem tricycle is similar in layout to that described for Plate 20 but in this version, the rear rider not only drives in a different way but has a much more pleasant view. The front wheel as in the previously mentioned model is standard boneshaker design, including as one can see foot-rests for the fast downhill run but the rear rider operates the rear cranked axle with both hands and feet. The feet were placed in special leather 'shoes' on the treadles fitted to the cranked axle and aided by two hand-held levers. When travelling downhill with the front rider neatly resting his feet on the rests, the position of the rear man avoiding flying hand levers must have been unenviable.

Plate 24 – Pickering's velocipede. 1868. This American-built machine owed a lot in design to the boneshakers imported into the United States at the time. The steering arm had a curious bend to it while the seat was slightly farther back than on the standard boneshaker. One curious and perhaps dangerous 'improvement' was the rear wheel brake. This was fitted to the underside of the saddle and poised over the tyre of the rear wheel. To apply the brake, the rider had to force his weight back and down into the saddle to allow the block to make contact. The possibility of accidental braking is obvious.

Plate 25 – Boneshaker bicycle. 1870. This machine is a transitional model between the true boneshaker and the later ordinary or 'Penny-Farthing' machine. In this model the rear wheel had diminished in size to save weight while the front wheel has increased in diameter to allow the rider to cover more ground with a single revolution of the pedals. Because of the increase in size of the front wheel and the difficulties of mounting, the manufacturer has thoughtfully fitted a small mounting step at the rear. This can be clearly seen.

Plate 26 – Ariel men's and ladies' bicycles. 1872. The Ariel introduced by James Starley was the first English ordinary machine and had the new and advanced lever tension spokes and wheels which were fitted with solid India rubber tyres. The advertisement also boasted of an 'Improved Rudder' and many other finer improvements. The machine and the others that followed it readily caught on and the size of the front wheel took much of the previous exertion out of cycling. Starley also saw the possibility of opening up the ladies' market and produced a side-saddle version with lever drive. Unfortunately, the idea never caught on and women had to content themselves with 'sociable' machines of a safer and more demure nature.

Plate 27 – Ordinary bicycle. 1880. This shows one of the large varieties of ordinaries produced by various manufacturers and local makers. They all conformed to the basic design of one large and one small wheel, direct pedalling and direct steering. The cycling boom that gripped England also invaded America. In the United States various manufacturers but mainly importers tried to woo clients to buy their machines with convincing arguments. The advertisement for the Columbia Ordinary from a contemporary New York newspaper stated that it was 'a practical machine for all except old and infirm. Better than a horse as it needs no oats; because on it you can ride more miles in a day over common roads than a horse can go'.

Plate 28 – Ordinary bicycle. 1880. This machine was made by the famous English maker William Keen who had his factory at the Angel Inn, Thames Ditton. Certain improvements had already started to be made on these machines and these included attempts to lighten the frame for increased speed. The indispensable small rear wheel mounting step can be clearly seen.

Plate 29 – Ordinary bicycle. 1882. Yet another small variation of this ubiquitous machine. In this version, the shape of the frame differs slightly from that shown in Plate 28. The front wheel while the same size has many more spokes and the handlebars are of a slightly different shape.

Plate 30 – Detail of rear brake. 1882. This close-up shows an ingenious roller brake fitted to a rear wheel of an ordinary. Most of the early ordinaries did not possess brakes and it was later that some but by no means all fitted this or another form of brake. In similar way as the boneshaker brake it was worked by twisting the handlebars which tightened the cord and applied the brake.

Plate 31 – Ordinary bicycle. 1885. This plate taken from a contemporary photograph shows a rider with foot on the mounting step in the prepare to mount position. There was some considerable skill in mounting and dismounting these machines and various contemporary books and manuals give a step-by-step lesson in the art. The machine illustrated was made by William Keen of Thames Ditton, Surrey.

Plate 32 – Singer Xtraordinary bicycle. 1878. The Singer machine was one of a number of transitional machines that bridged the gap between the ordinary and the safety machine. By slightly reducing the wheel diameter and placing the saddle slightly farther back, over the back wheel, an initial attempt was made to produce a lower machine with less dangers to the rider in case of accident. To compensate for this layout, the machine was fitted with levers working on cranks on the front hub. These levers allowed the cyclist to still propel the machine when sitting in a safer position.

Plate 33 – Rotary tricycle. 1878. This machine first produced in 1878 captured a wide part of the three-wheeled market and took over from the first of this type manufactured by James Starley in 1876 under the title the Coventry lever tricycle. The Rudge machine was powered by chain drive on the larger driving wheel and steering and stability were provided by the two smaller wheels. Despite its somewhat unorthodox appearance, this type of machine was immensely popular for about 10 years, until ousted by the more conventional style of tricycle.

Plate 34 – Quadrant tricycle. 1880. This chain-driven machine, remarkably modern for its age was produced in 1880. It embodies chain drive, front-wheel steering and brakes. In its earlier life, this machine was the form of transport of the Mayor of Wallingford in Oxfordshire. It represents an early form of all metal tricycle with chain drive yet still with the larger rear wheels and a somewhat complicated system at the front.

Plate 35 – American velocipede. 1869. This illustration taken from the contemporary magazine *Harpers Weekly* shows the Pickering velocipede in use in New York in 1869. The machine had the front wheel larger than the rear one and the cranks fitted to the front hub being a series of holes for pedal adjustment. The crooked steering bar was rather cumbersome but seems to have performed adequately. Braking was carried out by the rider leaning back and pressing down on the saddle with his backside, which in turn pushed the brake block on to the rear wheel. As can be imagined, this was hardly the ideal method considering the road surfaces of the period.

Plate 36 – Lawson safety bicycle. 1876. This machine patented by H. J. Lawson in 1876, which bore the registered name of 'safety', was in reality an ordinary in reverse. Lawson placed the large driving wheel at the rear, built a frame which connected this to the front and smaller wheel, and fitted a rudimentary handlebar and steering column and a saddle. The drive was by means of levers and cranks. The mechanics allowed the cyclist from his forward position to still operate the cranks on the rear wheel. While a step in the

176

right direction by virtue of the fact that it lowered the driver from his lofty and dangerous position it never really caught on.

Plate 37 – Shergold safety bicycle. 1876. This machine which appeared in the same year as the Lawson safety was a greater step towards the true safety bicycle than would appear within the next decade. Thomas Shergold had the machine locally made in Gloucester and except for the linked type steering arrangement embodied at least some of the points that would make up the later safety machine. The bicycle possessed chain drive and an adequate if somewhat heavy frame, a rear wheel brake (still boneshaker style) and a saddle mounted at a convenient and safe height. While the basic idea was there it needed the inventiveness and ingenuity of the manufacturers to turn it into a practical reality.

Plate 38 – Otto dicycle. 1880. The Otto dicycle was perhaps one of the strangest machines made at the time when manufacturers were desperately trying to snatch trade from their competitors. The machine consisted of two large wheels and very little else although some models – though not all – were fitted with a 'tail' with steadying wheel. The driving bar turned by the feet turned two independent wheels which transmitted the drive to the other two wheels at the hub. No chain was used but a steel belt. Balance had to be just right to avoid tipping backward or forward and in spite of this drawback about 1,000 were made and even a club of enthusiasts who called themselves 'Ottoists' sprang up.

Plate 39 – 'Kangaroo' dwarf ordinary bicycle. 1885. This was one of the many attempts and transitional machines between the ordinary and the safety machine. Like the Singer Xtraordinary, it is lower than the ordinary in the interests of safety. The machine while outwardly resembling an ordinary had the saddle set back but most important of all it incorporated chain drive, although the length of chain used was very little. As the rider's legs were nearer the ground than the hub of the front wheel where the drive was, the hub was connected by two chains, one each side of the wheel to a lower set of cogged wheels fitted to the frame to which the pedals were attached. One main and decided advantage was that the front wheel was geared up to compensate for the smaller diameter of the wheel.

Plate 40 – Hemming's unicycle. 1882. Richard Hemming of New Haven, Connecticut, U.S.A., designed this curious machine, one of many that either appeared in illustrations and were never built or were made in prototype form only. The inventor claimed that the machine could be propelled at 25 miles per hour by using both feet and arms. Stability would obviously be a problem!

Plate 41 – Rudge quad triplet. 1881. This unique machine with its four equal-sized wheels, a chain drive and rear driver direct drive was for its time a very advanced machine. As can be seen from the illustration foot-rests were still indispensable for fast travelling and a new improved style of brake took much of the danger out of speedy downhill runs.

Plate 42 – Bayliss and Thomas tandem tricycle. 1882. This machine is an example of one of the many styles of sociable machines made at this time. Another was the Rudge side-by-side quadricycle. This machine while having chain drive also had a lever band brake operated by the rear man and steering by the front man. The cranked driving axle at the front was connected by a chain to the driving wheel hub and the efforts of the rear man were transmitted to the hub of the opposite wheel by a similar chain.

Plate 43 – Warwick Monarch caddy. 1880. This highly sedate and impressive machine despite its looks and obvious connexion with bath chairs incorporated a number of advanced improvements from a mechanical point of view. The two-seater machine had the driving position at the front with cranked axle and foot-rests for propulsion and handles for steering the machine. There are two large wheels at the front and a single small wheel at the rear above which is mounted the resplendent wicker seat complete with wicker tube on the right side to hold an umbrella! The rear wheel is fitted with a simple form of coiled spring suspension to cushion the ride for the rear seat passenger.

Plate 44 – Detail of rear suspension. This close-up shows the coiled rear wheel suspension system and the rod link steering system from the front handles to the small rear steering wheel.

Plate 45 – Bayliss and Thomas folding tricycle. 1881. This most unusual tricycle was an effort to solve the storage problems of machines of this type. The layout is conventional with two large front wheels with a chain drive on the left wheel. The cranked axle has two pedals which transmits the power to a cogged wheel and this is connected to another cogged wheel at the hub by a chain. The brass plate on the frame is dated 9 March 1881 and proclaims that the machine was manufactured at the Folding Excelsior Works, Coventry.

Plate 46 – Bayliss and Thomas folding tricycle. 1881. This plate shows the tricycle in the folded position which allowed the owner to take it into the house if required or store it in a small space.

Plate 47 – Tricycle with double cogged gear. 1881. This machine shows an attempt to introduce gearing to tricycles and follows the accepted practice of having two larger front wheels and a small rear wheel. The usual cranked axle with foot-rests was fitted connected on the right side to a cogged wheel which connected with another which in turn worked on the cogged hub. Steering was by means of the two handles which connected with rods and links to the rear wheel.

Plate 48 – Starley tricycle. 1883. This illustration shows clearly the superior construction of the Starley machine. With its two large rear wheels and smaller front steering wheel it was immensely popular. Notice also the tiller arms at the rear with small wheel. This was fitted to most of this style of machine to prevent accidents from overbalancing. One of the refinements of this machine was the fitting at last of an efficient band brake.

Plate 49 – Carrouch tricycle. 1880. This shows yet another form of the popular tricycle but with a difference. This machine had a front gear system which can be seen on the left wheel and a rear steering wheel operated again by rods and link system. One of inherent dangers of this type of machine was the possibility of a forward tip. The Carrouch like others of its type enjoyed immense popularity amongst a certain sector of the cycling public and did not really start to disappear until the safety bicycle and tricycle came on the scene.

Plate 50 – Cheylesmore tricycle. 1880. This was a most popular machine and differs from the Carrouch previously described in having drive on both front wheels. The cranked axle fitted between the front portion of the frame has two pedals and a cogged wheel at each end. These cogged wheels are connected to cogs on the hubs by a continuous chain. Steering was by the usual rear wheel method connected by rods and links to the steering handles situated either side of the saddle.

Plate 51 – Coventry Machinists' tricycle. 1878. This popular machine for both men and women had a smaller front wheel with rods and links to the side steering handles and pedals fitted to the central frame connected by a continuous chain to an axle with a cogged wheel, on the ends of which were fitted the wheels. To avoid any nasty accidents by tipping back, the machine was fitted with a rear tiller and small wheel for steadying.

Plate 52 – Rudge Sociable tricycle. 1878. This plate shows a typical example of the many sociable tricycles, although sportier owners preferred the tandem arrangement for less wind resistance. This side-by-side model, ideal for a slow jaunt or promenade has both passengers doing an equal amount of work. The small front wheel was for steering and

180

was connected to two handles positioned each side of the saddle of the right-hand cyclist while the left-hand cyclist took charge of the brake lever. Chain guards were fitted and can be seen on the right wheel.

Plate 53 – Norfolk tricycle. 1888. This machine had treadles to transmit power to the large rear wheel and had a simple tiller to steer the front wheel. The smaller rear wheel was to balance the machine. This example was custom-made probably for a doctor as the various lockers fitted to it have ingenious locking systems suitable for the storing of medicines. Many country doctors and the clergy adopted this type of tricycle for ease and sedate riding in accord with their calling.

Plate 54 – Singer poster. 1880's. This is an example of the graphic style of cycle posters produced at this time. It shows in a country setting the various types of machines made by the company from the ordinary, the xtraordinary, sociables and tricycles to more sedate machines for ladies' use.

Plate 55 – Howe poster. This, another example of the style of poster of the period shows an elegant gentleman on his Howe tricycle with its chain drive, front wheel steering and impressive brake lever.

Plate 56 – Tandem tricycle. 1880's. This illustration from a contemporary photograph shows a dashing line in tandem tricycles preferred by the sportier of the cycling fraternity. Both riders pedalled and each set of pedals was connected to the driving cog on the axle by separate sets of continuous chains. The front rider was responsible for steering the machine. Many variations of this basic style were produced by a number of manufacturers.

Plate 57 – Rover safety bicycle. 1884. This illustration represents Starley's first attempt at producing a safety bicycle. The front wheel was still larger than the rear one and perhaps the most complicated part of the design was the indirect steering. The frame was still slightly reminiscent of the ordinary with the long downdropping portion behind the front wheel but it was braced across the top with the saddle frame and steering system. Not satisfied with his first attempt, Starley produced two further models before settling for the last one made.

Plate 58 – B.S.A. safety bicycle. 1884. This was an attempt by the arms manufacturers, the Birmingham Small Arms Company to get into the safety cycle market. They had previously manufactured the Otto dicycle but had stopped manufacture after making about 1,000 machines. Taking out a patent in 1884, they produced this machine mainly from tricycle parts and utilized rifle cleaning rods for the rod and link system. The rear wheel sported a mudguard and the power was transmitted from the pedals by a continuous chain.

Plate 59 – Humber safety bicycle. 1884. The Humber machine was perhaps the first to dispense with the single backbone frame and was the forerunner of the widely used and proved diamond frame. The bicycle had a small front wheel and large rear wheel with chain drive and also had an adjustable saddle and direct steering. The height of the handlebars was also adjustable and the rear wheel hub was still fitted with a mounting step! While the machine had many advantages over other primitive safetys it was soon to be eclipsed by Starley's improved model.

Plate 60 – Second Rover safety bicycle. 1885. This illustration shows Starley's second attempt at producing a safety machine. With the advice of others including a famous competition cyclist as well as a worker in the metal industry, Starley provided the machine with direct steering, adjustable saddle and raked head. Foot-rests were still provided on the front forks of the frame as was the mounting step on the rear fork. The saddle and mountings were slightly improved and although the machine was used in the famous 100 mile race in 1885, Starley was far from satisfied and produced yet another model which formed the prototype for the safety machine that was to soon flood the market the world over.

Plate 61 – Premier safety bicycle. 1885. This was yet another form of safety machine produced at this time. This machine had wheels of almost the same size and a frame construction which still clung to the old main backbone type but also incorporated a diamond–type frame with it. There was as usual now direct steering and an adjustable saddle. The machine was also fitted with a lever type brake that acted on the front wheel.

Plate 62 – Raleigh safety bicycle. 1888. This was the product of the firm of Raleigh which had a diamond–type frame with extra supporting strut, adjustable saddle and direct steering but with a larger rear wheel than front wheel. As can be seen comparing the above three plates there was little to choose from in new innovations and all safety types enjoyed a measure of success at this period, although the hard core of diehards continued with the ordinaries and dwarf ordinaries, tricycles and quadricycles.

Plate 63 – Singer carrier. 1885. This illustration represents the Singer carriers purchased by the *Evening Standard* to deliver their newspapers to the street vendors. Other trades also used the basic carrier adapted to their needs and illustrations show it carrying milk and as a general delivery van. While the basic design of the machine differed little from the sociable and single tricycles, the commercial uses were obvious but it was not until the safety that the delivery-tricycle became universally popular.

Plate 64 – Rudge quadricycle. 1888. This was one of a number of sociables, tandem or otherwise that developed from the introduction of the safety bicycle. There are two separate sets of drive chains, one for the front rider and another for the rear rider who was in mixed company nearly always the man. The steering was also done by the rear cyclist.

Plate 65 – Olympia tandem tricycle. 1890. This was yet another form developed from the safety, with the rear position of the machine being of safety construction. The front arrangement is similar to the Rudge shown in Plate 64. Both cyclists pedalled the machine.

Plate 66 – Rudge dual-control tricycle. 1890. This magnificent-looking machine was designed to take a lady at the front and a gentleman at the rear (note the shape of frame). This machine with longer than average wheelbase was designed perhaps for the elderly and more portly part of the cycling fraternity as the unique style of frame has another axle positioned just to the rear of the front saddle where two more wheels – making five in all – could be fitted to allow the frame to take extra weight. The steering was dual-control so that perfect co-ordination between the two riders was essential. While the lady rode in the front and in some way must have dictated the steering, the brake lever was fitted to the back set of handlebars.

Plate 67 – German Mergamobile. 1890. This ingenious and unique machine was the first machine that could be designated a universal bicycle as it was suitable for all ages from children upwards. In a slightly retrograde step, the frame is made from wood and the whole machine has a somewhat old-fashioned appearance for its age. However, the simple mechanics and ingenious pulley system were the advantages of the machine, although it is difficult to see the advantages of it over the now established safety. The two pedals fitted to the front forks were connected with cord, passing over one pulley and around the driving hub. The pedals were worked up and down to produce propulsion. The main feature of this system was that by altering the length of cord, the pedals could be adjusted to any height to suit the rider.

Plate 68 – Tricycle with solid tyres. 1900. This represents a typical tricycle at the turn of the century with sturdy frame, almost equal size wheels, lamp on the front, rear wheel brake and surprisingly no free wheel, there being foot rests provided fitted to the front forks. The handlebars are fitted with a single lever for rear wheel brake and a bell.

Plate 69 – Child's horse tricycle. 1890's. This illustration represents almost the original idea of the hobby horse but updated. The bicycle developed from the child's hobby horse is in this case a tricycle and instead of a normal frame a wooden horse has been used; the handlebars fitted behind the head of the horse emerge at the chest and divide to form the forks. The machine is front wheel direct drive, a system still used today on child's tricycles.

Plate 70 – Child's tricycle. 1890's. This plate shows the tricycle manufactured in the 1890's for the large children's market. With solid tyres and of simple construction, the machine had the standard front wheel direct-drive system, sprung seat and no brakes. The basic shape of the frame has altered little when one compares this with modern-made tricycles, although materials have changed.

Plate 71 – Child's tricycle. 1910. This machine has a slightly different style of frame than the tricycle shown in Plate 70 but in other respects has not altered in style of manufacture. This machine does not have the divided rear frame but a single curved tube frame connected to a cross tube to which the rear wheels were fitted. Once again the machine has front wheel direct drive no brakes but an adjustable saddle.

Plate 72 – Lawson's 'bicyclette'. 1879. This machine patented by Lawson in 1879 followed on from the machine he had patented in 1876 (see Plate 36). It was perhaps the first safety bicycle which embodied some of the later used ideas, while itself never becoming popular or getting the market it justifiably deserved. While still clinging to the large front and smaller rear wheel principle it did employ a simple form of frame with adjustable saddle, and pedals fitted to a cogged wheel connected to the rear hub by a continuous chain, a system which was soon to be universally adopted. To place the rider in a suitable and comfortable position, the handlebars were connected to the front fork for the steering by rod and links while the rear wheel brake was still the antique block type.

Plate 73 – Bamboo bicycle. 1895. This was one of a number of novelty machines manufactured in this period. Because of the large market and the equally large number of manufacturers with very identical products, some designers felt that the only way to attract attention to their machines was to in some way make them different. While following the accepted design and shape of the safety bicycle (this was done to facilitate the supply of components for the small manufacturer) the frame is made from male bamboo. Female bamboo was not suitable as it is partially hollow whereas male bamboo is solid. The Bamboo Cycle Co. Ltd, of Holborn Viaduct, London, announced in their advertisements that bamboo was better than steel, but they did not add in which way. If they meant it did not rust, they were undoubtedly right but if they meant stronger which one suspects they intended their customers to think, it certainly was not. Another such novelty machine, but possibly with more application was the American Chicago Ice Bicycle, again constructed on the lines of the safety but having a specially designed rear wheel fitted with devices to dig into the ice for rear wheel grip and the front wheel replaced by a small ski.

Plate 74 – Safety bicycle. 1893. This illustration taken from a contemporary photograph shows the radical Miss Reynolds of Brighton on a machine made by R. S. Lovelace. It shows an example of one of the safety machines made by small manufacturers, this one being fitted with drop–style handlebars. Miss Reynolds scandalized society by riding in rational dress from Brighton to London accompanied by a party of young men. What was her worst crime was not the dress or the accompanying men but that she rode a man's bicycle.

Plate 75 – Elswick lady's safety bicycle. 1896. This machine shows the lady's model made by the Elswick Company, the large ship building and cannon kings W. G. Armstrong. The illustration also shows the famed actress Mabel

Love and although she claimed to be a rider it is possible that this was an excellent advertising photograph put out by Elswick to popularize their products. The machine has a sturdy frame, chain case and netting over the rear wheel. The machine also has mudguards front and rear and a brake to the front wheel using lever and connecting rods to press a block of rubber on to the tyre. Both saddle and height of handlebar was adjustable.

Plate 76 – Military bicycle. 1896. This illustration taken from a contemporary photograph shows a soldier of the 13th Middlesex Volunteers Queen's Westminsters which was one of the regiments to follow the example of the 26th Middlesex Rifle Volunteers and form a cycle company. From the study of contemporary photographs it appears that there was no standard type of machine and any safety seems to have been pressed into service. It was not until later that special military style machines were made such as the B.S.A. folding military bicycle and the B.S.A. Territorial bicycle.

Plate 77 – Dursley Pedersen bicycle. 1904. This machine patented by Pedersen in 1893 was a radical departure from the hundreds of safety machines made by various manufacturers who all followed with perhaps slight small variations the established safety design. The triangular frame was of thinner lightweight tubes each one duplicated, and constructed in a triangular frame specially to withstand the stresses and the duplicated frame gave it torsional stiffness. The other radical departure was the hammock-style saddle. This was made from netting and suspended between handlebars and rear portion of the frame. The saddle was adjustable and could be made tighter or slacker depending on the rider. A lady's model was also manufactured with a slightly different saddle arrangement to eliminate the stretch from handlebars to rear portion of the frame; this was accomplished by fitting an extra pair of forks at the back and the hammock-style saddle was suspended between these and the main rear part of the frame. The lady's model was also fitted with a chain case. A unique child's model exists and it is thought that this was specially made for Pedersen's son.

Plate 78 – Safety bicycle. 1900. This illustration represents the typical safety bicycle taken out to South Africa during the Boer War for the cyclist volunteers who went out there. They were used for scouting and by despatch riders and on the open veldt were a useful addition to mobility.

Plate 79 – Kendrick tricycle. 1914. This machine is a radical departure from the usual layout of the tricycle. In this case the machine possessed a large rear wheel of conventional size with frame and saddle reminiscent of the current safety machine but had two smaller wheels at the front. The ingenious steering rods and links can be clearly seen in the illustration and another advanced feature is the rear wheel brake operated by Bowden cable.

Plate 80 – Sociable tricycle. 1914. Although the true side-by-side sociable had been mostly abandoned in favour of the tandem because of the width of the machine, some examples of curious construction were made. The illustration shows one such machine. This construction employed the rear parts of two safety machines, one for gentlemen and the other for ladies and fitted these together giving it a central front steering wheel. While both sides were fitted with handlebars and pedalling was done by both parties, the steering was in the hands of the gentleman. Once again a system of links and rods was used and these can be clearly seen in the illustration. The rear wheel brake was also in the capable hands of the gentleman.

Plate 81 – Crypto Bantam bicycle. 1896. This machine was the last adults' bicycle with direct pedal drive to the front wheel. The gearing was in the front wheel hub and the pedals fitted to it. A child's model was also manufactured and while enjoying moderate success, it was unable to resist the tide of popularity enjoyed by the safety.

Plate 82 – Rover shaft-drive bicycle. 1910. This illustration shows one of the attempts to introduce alternative drive to the continuous chain. While outwardly conforming in frame design to the conventional safety, the use of the shaft drive did away with the need for chain and large cogged driving wheel. Encased in a tube, the shaft with suitable gearing occupied little room. A number of manufacturers turned to this new form of propulsion including Fabrique Nationale d'Armes de Guerre in Liège, Durkoppwerk A. G. of Reinckendorf, and a number of other companies. While it enjoyed a moderate success, its life was fairly short-lived and it disappeared in the 1920's. Its demise was due to the fact that it offered no advantage over the conventional chain-driven safety while costing more. As in every form of invention, it attracted those who wished to be individualists.

Plate 83 – Rover shaft-drive lady's bicycle. 1910. This is the lady's version of the shaft-driven Rover described in Plate 82.

Plate 84 – Detail of shaft drive. This illustration shows the simplicity and uncluttered appearance of the totally enclosed shaft drive.

Plate 85 – Ariel quint. 1896. This was one of the varied multiple tandems produced in this period. Ideal for touring and racing, they found a popular market amongst the sportier members of the cycling fraternity. This style of machine came in two-seater, three-seater and four- and five-seaters, although six and even more seats are known, one of the largest being the Quatrodecimalopede which was over 30 foot long.

Plate 86 – Ladies' tricycle. 1912. This is a prime example of the conventional tricycle of the pre-World War I period which enjoyed a wide following amongst ladies and more staid and elderly gentleman. With its small shopping basket on the front it was a sedate form of transport which required little effort and no chances of an indiscreet tumble.

Plate 87 – Chater Lea tandem. 1910. This illustration shows one of the most popular forms of touring machine manufactured – the tandem. With its long wheelbase, two sets of pedals and chains, and front wheel steering it was an ideal machine for weekend exploration of the countryside and was popular in many countries. Various makers appreciated this vast market and produced various types conforming in general to this type of design. Tandem riding had its own skill and perfect co-ordination between the two riders when it came to balance or cornering was essential.

Plate 88 – Chater Lea pacing machine. 1898. With the increased popularity in cycle racing both as a spectator sport and a testing ground for manufacturers, machines like this were produced as pacing bicycles for the cycling stars. The trainer or pace rider with an easy to ride highly geared machine – this example has a 20 in. geared wheel – started out on the track with the racing cyclists following and without too much skill or effort on his behalf set the speed for the training sessions. This machine, while conforming in some ways to the safety commercial bicycle has been stripped of all unnecessary weight including brakes.

Plate 89 – Ladies' safety bicycle. 1912. This illustration shows a typical lady's safety machine of the period and a design that was followed for some decades afterwards and can still be seen in some rural and country districts now in daily use. It has all the refinements including a net over the rear wheel, sedate drop frame, lamp on the front and enclosed chain case and brake. For more mundane outings a shopping basket could be fitted in place of the lamp at the front.

Plate 90 – Triumph safety with side-car. 1912. This geared machine – note the change switch on the crossbar – has been fitted with a wicker side-car and extra wheel. This was a very popular form of machine for two people who perhaps were not daring enough to brave the two-wheeled tandem but it did allow travel if perhaps two bicycles could not be afforded or if one of the riders was not a cyclist. The wicker chair also doubled as a useful shopping basket.

Plate 91 – Raleigh Carefree with wicker trailer. 1912.
This shows another alternative for carrying two people but unlike the previous example which was manufactured in that form, this machine was a safety with the added trailer. These trailers could be hired for 1s. (5p) per week to take girl friend, mother, etc. on a jaunt in town or country. They were extremely popular with courting couples if finances only allowed one machine and temporary conversion into a two-person machine was more practical than a permanent two seater.

Plate 92 – Referee safety bicycle. 1901. This shows one of the many varied safety machines on the market at the turn of the century. The referee machine had a slightly different design of frame to other machines with double style of crossbar but it still proved very popular. In later years, many of these individual manufacturers because of the slump in cycles either ceased manufacture or were taken over by larger concerns who used their names in some cases but not all and standardized design.

Plate 93 – Milk delivery tricycle. 1910. This is a prime example of the safety used for commercial purposes. In this case the machine shown was used in Benson many years ago for delivery of milk direct from the churn. The present owner can remember seeing this machine when he was a boy. The rear part is pure safety bicycle parts but the front frame is designed specially to hold the 'cart' for the churn with wheels fitted each side. The G.P.O. also used such machines with red wicker baskets on the front for parcel delivery.

Plate 94 – Delivery tricycle. 1914. This shows another application of the safety for delivery purposes, this time a medical publisher and bookseller of London. This form of closed box type delivery tricycles were very popular for use by commercial bodies such as publishers, hatters, wine merchants, etc. to deliver their orders in congested town and cities. This form was also used later by ice cream vendors but never caught on with butchers or greengrocers who preferred the two-wheeled machines with bracket on the front for basket and boxes.

Plate 95 – Golden Sunbeam safety bicycle. 1915. This shows one of the more famous of safety machines which were produced during the heyday of bicycles before the upsurge in recent times. The Golden Sunbeam was in the so-called luxury class of machine where attention to every detail in manufacture produced an outstanding but expensive machine. Patronized by the wealthier, the Golden Sunbeam remained unaltered in design from its introduction in 1902 until its demise in 1936. It was an outstanding example of craftsmanship and reliability.

Plate 96 – Tricycle. 1910. This shows another form of tricycle so popular at this period with two smaller wheels at the rear and a conventional normal sized safety wheel at the front. These were made in many styles and a number of sizes for the growing youthful market.

Plate 97 – Folding B.S.A. bicycle. 1915. This slightly unusual example of a folding bicycle dated 1915 is a conventional safety with quick release folding mechanism built into it. In common with the usual style of this machine, only a front wheel brake was fitted. The stand on which the machine is sitting was a later civilian addition. One is tempted to think that this form of folding machine was designed in this way for ease of production whereas later folding army bicycles (see Plate 99) were specially made to a special design.

Plate 98 – Folding B.S.A. bicycle, folded. 1915. This shows the machine folded for storage or more usually for carriage. The machine was by means of leather or webbing straps slung on the back of the soldier.

Plate 99 – B.S.A. folding military bicycle. 1940. This shows the development of the military cycle adapted for folding use and made with lightweight frame for ease of carriage. These and also 'trade' bicycles – normal commercial machines – were used by airborne troops. To fold this machine, the frame has to be unhinged by means of two wing nuts. While slower than the quick release mechanism on the cycle shown in Plate 97, this machine had the advantage of less weight. It was as was common in the late 1930's fitted with front and rear brakes.

Plate 100 – Kendrick racing tricycle. 1930's. This shows the perfection to which the tricycle had risen by this time. With down drop handlebars, rear and front brakes activated by Bowden cable, its lightweight frame and front wheel steering system, it represented the last word in the racing and civilian machine. The front left brake was even fitted with a lock which needed a key to free the brake to allow the machine to be ridden.

Plate 101 – Indian soldier with military bicycle. 1916. This illustration taken from a contemporary photograph shows an Indian havildar or sergeant with his bicycle loaded with rifle in waterproof cover and waterproof roll on the front. The bicycle is a B.S.A. Territorial, much favoured before World War I by the cyclist battalions of the Territorial army. The machine has a single front brake operated by lever and rods and a rack above the rear wheel for extra carrying space. Many of these machines, adapted for military use were shipped to France and found use mainly out of the front line for despatch riders, troop movements, etc. but the motorcycle and lorry were more in evidence and slowly were to oust the bicycle as a serious military form of transport until World War II when it was used by airborne and other troops.

Plate 102 – Types of saddles. This illustration shows two of the many and varied types of saddles, designed and used or designed and forgotten that the accessory makers attempted to market. The left-hand saddle is a pneumatic saddle with internal tube or bladder blown up to suit the cyclist with air from a normal tyre pump. On the right is a rocker saddle fitted to the frame and sprung but designed to give a rocking movement when riding along. This it was claimed eased the hardness of the roads and made a more comfortable ride.

Plate 103 – Cycle lamps. Cyclometers. Tyre pump.
This illustration shows a variety of cycle accessories including a selection of cycle lamps of all types and two cyclometers, the one on the left designed for night as well as day work by having a bell that rang once every mile was completed. The cyclometer was invented and manufactured first in Switzerland. In the centre is a cycle pump. This conveniently shaped necessity had a clamp to hold it shut but when opened only needed connecting and then the top could be pushed up and down with foot or hand.

Plate 104 – Plaques of cycle manufacturers. This illustration shows a variety of plaques fitted to the front steering tube of cycles by various manufacturers and most of these shown are now extinct. These colourful and often ornate and decorative metal plaques have now given way to ordinary transfers.

Plate 105 – Peugeot Sports special. 1977. The Peugeot sports special is a typical example of a sport bicycle today. It is similar in design to their tourer but with stainless steel mudguards. It is equipped with centre pull brakes and come in either five- or ten-speed versions, and a frame in three sizes. The wheels are 27 in. diameter.

Plate 106 – Peugeot gents' tourer. 1977. This is another typical example of the modern safety bicycle with added refinements of dynamo-driven lamp and derailleur gears.

Plate 107 – Peugeot ladies' sports. 1977. This machine with its modern frame design is equipped with ten-speed derailleur gears, dynamo lighting and large flange quick release hubs. It is typical of the modern attention to detail in cycles made today.

Plate 108 – Raleigh Chopper. 1977. This universal cycle is the result of modern design and research applied to the traditional safety bicycle. With Sturmey-Archer three-speed gear and suspension under the saddle plus its novel design, it shows everything that modern design and industry has done to change the image of the bicycle and to modernize it. One notes that the rear wheel is larger than the front wheel.

Plate 109 – Raleigh Scrambler Trike. 1977. This shows the modern tricycle made for the four- to five-year-old range of the market and with its direct pedal drive to the front wheel and shape of frame it is interesting to compare it with the child tricycles shown in Plates 70 and 71.

Plate 110 – Raleigh Nova bicycle. 1977. This shows the modern lightweight and small bicycle so popular today because of size which is easy to ride and store. The Nova has a three-speed Sturmey-Archer gear with controls on the handlebars with gear and brake cable for the rear wheel concealed in the tube frame. Because of its design and versatility with adjustable height to handlebars and saddle it is truly as the makers claim an all-family machine.

Plate 111 – Raleigh Strika. 1977. This shows yet another new style of cycle available today which with front suspension thick tread tyres and handlebar shape owes more perhaps to racing and dirt track motor cycles than bicycles but with its front wheel brakes and adjustable saddle and handlebars it is the shape of cycle that children and youngsters have come to expect.

Plate 112 – Bickerton folding bicycle. 1977. This is perhaps the latest in the small wheeled folding machines that evolved from the original Moulton design. The versatility of the machine is astounding being adjustable to fit a child right up to a 6 ft 2 in. adult. Weighing a mere 18 lbs it can be folded and carried in a special holdall. Various versions are made, that intended for town use only – ideal for London and other congested cities – has a single speed (sixty-five gear) while the tourer is equipped with the Sturmey-Archer three-speed hub.

Plate 113 – Raleigh Stowaway. 1977. This again shows how the modern small cycle can be made to fold easily and be conveniently stored.